SAINTS FOR TODAY

IVAN INNERST

SAINTS FOR TODAY
Reflections on lesser saints

IGNATIUS PRESS   SAN FRANCISCO

Cover art by Christopher J. Pelicano
Cover design by Riz Boncan Marsella

© 2000 Ignatius Press, San Francisco
ISBN 0–89870–782–x
Library of Congress catalogue number 99–68077
Printed in the United States of America ∞

For my wife, Betty,
and our children and grandchildren

The saints included within these pages are not to be thought of as lesser in holiness, or less deserving of veneration, than others of their sanctified communion. They simply are generally less well known than those saints for whom are reserved the major feasts. Yet in each case they have much of value to say for the Church, and to the world, today.

Contents

THE CHOICE

Ralph Milner

THE Communion of Saints has never been more indispensable for the safe passage of the Church than it is today, when the Barque of Peter is besieged by such heavy seas from without and threatened by mutiny from within.

During those tempest-tossed periods in her earthly voyage, the Church has always turned, as to a compass, to her saints. And should certain times call for the support or the assistance of particular saints, what a richly diverse company she has from which to choose!

The saints would appear to share but a single trait: holiness. For the rest, their very appeal may lie at least somewhat in their unlikeness. They have been scholars and slaves, kings or queens and beggars, old men and young girls, the gregarious and solitaries who have dwelt in deserts and caves, the golden-tongued and those vowed to silence, the eccentrics and the wholly mainstream.

Who then might we pose as one saint for now?

There is a sanctified soul I propose who is so obscure he is not even granted his own special entry in Alban Butler's *Lives of the Saints* but must rest content with being included in the company of "Blessed Roger Dickenson and his Companions". This man bears the unceremonious name of Ralph Milner. He was English and lived in the sixteenth century, the heralded Elizabethan Age in England, a Renaissance period of Shakespearean grandeur, when Catholics, however, were not tolerated, and more than a few now beatified or canonized were hunted down, often tortured and put to death.

Even more important for us moderns, Milner was an illiterate farmer. He was a Protestant who, impressed by the lives of those Catholics he observed, converted to the Catholic faith. He was found out and imprisoned almost at once, after his First Communion, but was later, on more than one occasion, set free, each time only to be jailed again. A more prudent man might then have let well enough alone and remained free. But saints are not known for practicing this sort of prudence. Each time upon his release, Milner worked to gain assistance for those Catholics still imprisoned or helped to conceal the missionary priests who were forced underground to survive. He was arrested a last time with one such priest, named Roger Dickenson, with whom he was brought to trial and whose feast day he shares on July 7 in the calendar of saints.

It is here, inside a sixteenth-century trial chamber, that we must pause to marvel today at such a sight as that which unfolded, where was displayed so great a show of loyalty and devotion to the Church and to Rome. The judge took pity on Milner, now elderly and a father of eight, and made him an offer so seemingly inoffensive, so benign, as to appear wholly acceptable for one whose very life hung on his answer. Milner, the judge ruled, had only to walk through the door, pass along the street, and enter a nearby Anglican church. This, he said, would constitute an act of reconciliation, and Milner would be at liberty to return to his family. That was to be all, the whole of it: a few short steps, the performance of an altogether symbolic act, and his life would be spared.

The question raised is an insistent one, and utterly human. Why could not Milner have agreed to the judge's well-meaning proposal yet remained a "secret Catholic" in his heart? In modern parlance, why should he have not accepted the offer while crossing his fingers behind his back? But the outcome of the story is, of course, evident. The man was a saint, after all, and there are no "secret Catholics" within that communion. Ralph Milner chose rather to stand stead-fast inside that chamber, and he was executed with Father Dickenson on July 7, 1591. He was quoted as responding to the judge: "Would your lordship then advise me, for the perishable trifles of this world, or for a wife and children, to lose my God? No, my lord, I cannot approve or embrace a counsel so disagreeable to the maxims of the Gospel."

The awesome choice made by Ralph Milner seems the greatest folly for those of us who live all these four hundred years later. It is somehow beyond our poor power to compre-hend, creatures as we are of this more enlightened, religiously tolerant age. Yet it ought not to be taken casually today by the faithful of the Western world, in this time of cafeteria Ca-tholicism, of freewheeling theology, of dissident clergy within the Church, of a too-often diffident laity. Nor should his words fall meaninglessly on the ear of the lukewarm within the fold of the Church: those who would scarcely think twice before performing so otherwise innocent an act as to step out one door and in through another, should that move spare for them "the perishable trifles of this world", and even though it cost them their Catholic faith.

This has nothing to do with a call for a return to the tooth-and-claw internecine church warfare of former times, which all civilized nations now deplore. Protestants in such societies no longer execute Catholics for being Catholic, nor do Catholics put to death Protestants for their reformist beliefs. It has everything to do with restoring among present-day Catholics an enduring loyalty to their Church and her teaching at one more period in her history when that Church is so beset both from within her ranks and from without by the secular world.

There is an added element to the story of this saint that we would today ignore at our spiritual peril. As has been noted, Milner was an illiterate farmer. Then should we not further ponder over how it is so much within our urban culture, among the sophisticated elite of our great cities and inside the halls of academe, that the secularism and heterodoxy we observe all around us have taken the deepest root? Is it not there that the believing, traditional Catholic is looked upon as little more than a well-meaning but misguided fool, blind to the ways of the modern world and blundering down some medieval path that leads backward into a discarded history?

That being the case, we would do well to rethink how we might better follow the lead of the "illiterate farmers" of this day and age who, in their simplicity of life and thought, their elemental wisdom and courage, could teach us a great deal indeed about the timeless qualities of the faith. They are, after all, as we have been told, the "little ones" to whom have been confided the mysteries of the Kingdom.

It has been rightly declared that the history of the Church is the history of her saints. We might therefore ask, caught within the throes of the present age: Blessed Ralph Milner, pray for us.

THE REAL PRESENCE

Paschal Baylon

T HE sight was an odd one to behold when it happened, and on holy ground. So unrestrained an outpouring of devotion was scarcely ordinary behind those walls, and surely it would have been thought to border on the eccentric.

As one friar watched, from where he was himself unobserved, the second friar performed an elaborate dance, moving his body back and forth, then leaping high into the air. But this was no simple show of agility. Nor had it anything to it of the artistic creation: the practiced moves, the graceful step. There was nothing of a choreographed stage performance to it, to be seen within a darkened theater.

It took place, rather, within the solemn confines of a monastery. More than this, it was in the dining hall in which the second friar, now the solitary dancer, served as refectorian. And the object of this unbridled display of emotion, which caused the simple friar to leap through the air? The refectory statue of Our Lady. It was wholly for her this obscure lay brother, believing he was alone, exhibited so great a show of affection and homage, a love he could no longer conceal, which burst forth with all the exuberance of a primitive dance.

The first friar, sole witness to so curious and uncommon a spectacle, was to slip out quietly, still unobserved, only to return to the dining hall later, after having reported to the other brothers he met that the friar-turned-dancer displayed a "radiant countenance".

This near-bizarre moment, scarcely more than a faded footnote in Church history, can yet serve as the best possible introduction to the one who acted out, with such unbounded fervor, his deepest feelings of pure devotion for all that was held to be sacred. It was this same passion that, in one form or another, was to distinguish this particular Franciscan lay brother's entire life, a trait that would lead one day to his being named by the Church, for all the world, the "saint of the Eucharist".

He was Paschal Baylon, and he was born in Aragon in 1540, the son of farm parents. From his earliest childhood, we are told, he displayed those characteristics expressive of what he was to become, something of the future refectory dancer. During his formative years and as a youth, till he was twenty-four, he was a shepherd, tending first his father's flock and then that of a rich landowner in the area. His was a solitary, some would say lonely, life. He lived in the open, where an ordinary youth might spend the long idle hours plotting for the day when he should escape from such boredom into the city and its pleasures. But if he were Paschal Baylon, he would, in this pastoral silence beneath the blue sky, become reflective and see around him the presence of God in His quietude.

It is here in this outdoor setting that a second glimpse into the life of the saint is given us, a sort of tableau altogether as illustrative of the man-to-be as any from inside the monastery walls. In this case it is the shepherd youth observed, who, since he could not abandon his sheep to go to church, knelt where he was for long periods in prayer, his eyes fixed on a distant sanctuary where Mass was being offered. From this hillside slowly emerged the first likeness, the prayerful image, of the future friar.

All, however, was not reflection or prayer. He was not every moment on his knees. For he wished to learn—and his only school was the outdoors and his only "schoolmates" the sheep. So he took a book with him into the fields, where he begged anyone who passed by to teach him the alphabet from its pages. And so it was that in time he learned to read.

Pious reflection first, then learning; there could be little doubt where he was headed, that he was not always to be a shepherd. In 1564 he began his life as a religious, having petitioned the Franciscans for admission into their order. As might be expected, he entered one of the strictest of the Franciscan orders, the friars of the Alcantarine reform. He with set purpose avoided the well-to-do monasteries. "I was born poor, and I am resolved to die in poverty and penance", he was to declare.

More than three centuries later, another holy figure, the sainted Pope Pius X, was to record in strikingly similar fashion when writing his last will and testament: "I was born poor, I have lived in poverty, and I wish to die poor." The simple friar and the holy pontiff in the Vatican, while so apart in time and station, were thus fully joined in their practice of true Christian poverty.

For Paschal Baylon, the austere life he chose to lead was not the sole sign of his humility. He chose as well never to become a priest, and he served all his days as a lay brother. He was in turn a cook, mendicant, gardener, and porter; and in every case he showed himself to be a man of great kindness, a healer for those less fortunate, and a worker of so many miracles that at his canonization hearing a cardinal is said to have cried out, "The like has never been seen!"

The like has never been seen.

Still, it is not his miracles or his kindness or his healing powers that we are privileged to remember for our own edification in this present moment, standing as we do within the ruins wrought by a century and more of modernism. For indeed such virtues or powers have been possessed to one degree or another by different saints throughout the two thousand years of Christendom. Save for those martyred, simply to be canonized a saint requires the performance of miracles.

What makes Saint Paschal Baylon special and a needed model for Catholics today is that he remains, for the Church of Rome, the saint of the Eucharist.

We have already watched the young Paschal, as a shepherd, kneeling in prayer to face the distant sanctuary where Mass was being offered. That rustic scene serves only as sign of what was to come. The youth grown into manhood lost none of the fervid devotion for the Eucharistic Body that had so marked his earlier years. His was a total abandonment to the Real Presence, his fervor made manifest, it is said, by ecstasies and raptures no less profound than that spirit which moved him to perform his dance in homage before the statue of Our Lady. The dance and his prayer were one and the same.

Despite his many time-consuming monastic duties, he more often than not spent much of the night in prayer before the altar. He was to be found for long hours upon his knees before the tabernacle. He knelt without support, his two hands clasped and raised before his face. Every minute when he was not at his duties or before the Blessed Sacrament, Paschal spent in church, serving Mass after Mass as though he could not bear even for this long to be gone from the Presence made real on the altar before him in the hands and by the solemn words of the priest.

Even on his infrequent journeys outside the monastery walls, he seemed destined to make his devotion to the Blessed Sacrament known, and at least once at the risk of his life. This time, while he was travelling on an assignment through France, he was accosted by militant Huguenots, who then questioned him on this very matter. He responded at once and apparently so skillfully that the militants proceeded to stone him. The saint, however, escaped and went his way.

But nothing in his life so well defines Paschal Baylon as the circumstances surrounding his death, which occurred one day after his fifty-third birthday. It was as if, should he not be able to go to the altar, the Real Presence would instead come to him, as tribute to his lifelong spirit of devotion. Saint Paschal died just as the bell tolled from the chapel announcing the Consecration at the High Mass.

That zeal he displayed before the Sacred Mysteries was not to go unheeded by the Church. Pope Leo XIII proclaimed him "special patron of congresses and other Eucharistic associations".

The saint's shadow would seem to fall about every altar, here and now, around the world, where all these years later the faithful, of whom so many are no longer true believers, have gathered. The same shadow should spread into every sanctuary where today the Mass is considered little more than a social gathering of the community, where a common meal shall again be shared.

That shadow might serve as a holy and timely reminder of this saint as spiritual model for those who have come together forgetful of the sanctified air they breathe within these walls, or careless of the consecrated ground beneath their feet. Too often they have transformed that place, that ground, into Anywhere, a desacralized hall with little of mystery about it, of candlelight or statuary, of the darkened corner where one might kneel alone to pray. All may come and go about the altar or tabernacle with sparse sign of reverence or awe for what is so near, within their very reach. Though why ought they show any such regard for what is no longer "out there", just beyond their touch? Although God is both Mystery and Presence, His most visible signs have been removed, or reduced to the level of the common, the everyday.

The priest at the altar is no longer the celebrant of that great thanksgiving feast of sacrifice. He is the "presider" found at the town dinner or banquet, the master of ceremonies, as it were, a necessary figure whose role is primarily to see that the proper procedures are followed, that all may run smoothly.

Should we indeed wonder at what we have been told, what comes to us in the news of the day: a rising number of those in this land who each week partake of Communion no longer believe in the Real Presence of Him whom they nonetheless receive in their hand or upon their tongue?

A scandal, perhaps. But why any surprise? They will again be found each week or holy day in the line that makes its way slowly forward at Mass for what they now consider bread-as-symbol. There is the man with both hands thrust inside his pockets and the woman who greets a friend on the way. There are those who glance about, who have a roving eye for any small distraction, for what can entertain or amuse. It could as well be the line formed outside a movie theater. Though in such a line, perhaps, there might be a greater sense of anticipation!

The Communion line moves forward, in what has become for so many a simple practice of habit, and one is saddened to recall the oft-repeated story of the Protestant who remarked to his Catholic friend: "If I truly believed what you Catholics say you believe, I would go up for Communion on my knees!"

The French Catholic writer François Mauriac has written that, for him, in the Eucharist, "God has not answered my questions laden with despair: He has simply given Himself to me."

He gave Himself to Paschal Baylon, who was indeed a man on his knees before the Real Presence, unmindful of place and time with so great a Mystery before him. There has grown up a legend around this holy friar, one that refers to "Saint Paschal's knocks". The knocks are the sounds that make his presence known to those for whose salvation he fears. In his work *The Lives of the Saints*, the priest-historian and hagiographer Omer Englebert writes of these knocks:

> Sometimes strong and violent, these signs provoke terror; sometimes soft and gentle, they bring hope; sometimes they are simple and clear like awaited answers or friendly warnings. They have often called to order those who are lacking in respect for the consecrated Host.[1]

---

[1] Omer Englebert, *The Lives of the Saints* (New York: Barnes and Noble, 1994), 191–92.

THE HIDDEN LIFE

Rosalia

THEN what are we to make of her? This uncommon woman, Rosalia?

She confounds us the moment we try to grasp who she was, for someone so elusive at once slips from our hands. We can only imagine her look of disapproval, and even of sorrow, that we should so much as utter her name.

And if we should praise her, the praise proper for any saint? If we were to remark on her so intrepid spirit of self-abnegation—the role she chose to assume, that of "no one at all"? She would consider such praise to be an unintended unkindness. Those words of esteem would but attest, in her eyes, that the life she had vowed to live had come to nothing, a failure in the mind of another, by one's very acknowledgment of her existence!

Rosalia is for us, then, a true enigma. Though we would want to know of her, who is a saint, she in turn desires one thing only, that we know nothing about her, that she might be left in her blessed obscurity. She is the archetypical saint in the shadows, the retiring saint of legend, the one fearful of finding his glory among men, that acclaim which others so avidly seek. Rosalia is best described as that sanctified soul whose life, in the words of Saint Paul, is "hidden with Christ in God".

Then it is hardly to be thought strange if we should not feel a genuine sense of regret for thus intruding upon her solitude, the seclusion she sought with so great an ardor. Why would we not excuse ourselves, beg her forgiveness for seeking her out as a sign for a world that so worships celebrity, that bends its knee so shamelessly before the famous and near-famous and the merely notorious, the crude and outspoken, the *glitterati* of the earth?

It was from just such a world, one of power, that the saint herself fled. For she was not born into the lower classes, into simple or modest surroundings, but rather was a child of the court, that of Roger II, king of Sicily, about the year 1130. Her bloodline was nothing if not royal. As daughter of a man named Sinibald, "Lord of Roses and Quisquina", she was a descendant of Charlemagne himself.

She knew, then, of the trappings, the life spent in the best circles, so prized by the world. She knew them first as a child, from her earliest, most impressionable years: the favors given to those of a royal line, the obeisance shown them, the foremost place granted them in social rank. These court customs she surely observed all around her, in her own quarters and beyond. And to add to the rest, she was said to possess a striking beauty. So she would be thought an unusual girl indeed if she was not vain, accepting as due to her all that passed into her hands.

The histories of those medieval queens, and later saints, who gave up just such a court life upon the deaths of their husbands to assume the habit of a religious are better known to us. Perhaps because of their number, they have come to be thought of as not uncommon—the result of a peculiar "mind-set" to be found within the religiously charged atmosphere of the Middle Ages. There were, to name but two, the saints Elizabeth of Portugal and Elizabeth of Hungary. Upon giving up the throne, they both became tertiaries in the Third Order of Saint Francis. The first retired to a convent of Poor Clares. Such examples as these, of what we might today derisively call "downward mobility", are then to be found in that earlier age, those times we have come to regard as quaint or curious and thoroughly pious, an age replete with knights in armor, religious crusades, and mendicant friars.

But Rosalia?

Not for her so "narrow" a move as from court to convent, or so "modest" a change of dress as from royal purple to simple habit. This future saint left her royal quarters under cover of night, scarcely more than a child of fourteen, to live in a cave, where she wished to remain completely hidden from the world. She remained there but several months before she fled to a second cave, near Palermo. This was, we are told, either because she was informed by angels her parents were coming to look for her, or because her sought-for solitude was destroyed by petitioners who had found her out. Whatever the reason, it was into the second cave that she then vanished as though from off the face of the earth. The solitary sign we are given of her presence are these words discovered years later inscribed upon the walls of the cave, a simple pledge, yet one so eloquent in its way that it leaves all else better left unsaid: "I, Rosalia, daughter of Sinibald, Lord of Roses and Quisquina, have taken the resolution to live in this cave for the love of my Lord, Jesus Christ."

The inscription, so silent and personal a vow, was meant perhaps to be something of an epitaph, and the cave, her tomb, inside which she would die to the world, the very letters themselves to be at last erased by the passage of time so that not even this much, these few words, would be found to attest to her existence on earth. She would be known but to God. Not the slightest trace of her would remain. This was to be the last of it, the triumph of so great a humility that no one, least of all those she had once known, would hear of her again.

But fate would have it otherwise. Here was to be an ironic fate, as though God in His mysterious way had known all along what Rosalia could not have known, that He would make use of her to reveal to those ages yet to come the heights of sanctity to which such a humble soul as she could ascend.

She died alone, it is believed around 1160, when she was but thirty years of age. Her body was undiscovered for centuries, till it was found during the seventeenth century encased in the rock crystal of the cave. Found there too were what would seem to have been her sole possessions: a crucifix, a Greek cross made of silver, and a string of beads believed to be an early rosary.

The events that led to the discovery of the saint's remains were the primary cause of her "undoing". A plague swept through Palermo in 1624. One plague victim had a vision of Rosalia, a search was conducted, and the find was made in the nearby grotto. Her bones were placed in a reliquary and carried in procession through the streets of the city. The plague, so it was reported, was soon ended.

The reclusive saint's centuries-long hidden life "with Christ in God" was ended as well. She was to receive in death the very veneration and acclaim she had gone to such profound lengths to avoid during her life. Thus it was to come about that she was made patroness of Palermo, and Pope Urban VIII entered her name in the Roman martyrology. The faithful of Palermo to this day celebrate two feasts in her honor, one of which was elevated to the rank of a holy day by Pope Pius XI in 1927.

See how one writer describes the homage paid each year by those same faithful to this most solitary and retiring of holy women. There takes place, he writes,

> a procession of unequalled magnificence, heralded by cannon fire. The saint's shrine, atop a gigantic carriage filled with musicians, is drawn through the town by forty mules, accompanied by prayers, hymns and acclamations. The top of the carriage is level with the roofs of the houses; fireworks are set off everywhere; the musicians blow ceaselessly on their trumpets; and for the five days during which this celebration lasts, enthusiasm mounts to an increasingly high pitch.[1]

With just such splendor and pomp has the deafening silence of the lonely grotto been shattered, and we are again left to wonder at the ways of the world and those of sainthood: how God seeks to teach His creation in a manner we poor mortals shall never fully fathom.

Then what are we to make of Saint Rosalia? The woman confounds us in our minds and souls, where we are in the deepest sense human. For is there anyone who would not wish to be remembered, at least by a few, if for nothing more than some good he has rendered? Does this not help account, say, for the fact a man will rear his children so as to leave some trace of himself on earth? Here, then, is to be found a most elemental side of our nature, and hardly a side of which one ought be ashamed or that is lacking in virtue.

This much understood, we have nonetheless a lesson to learn from the strange, and remarkable, life of Rosalia. We can be grateful that this humble saint's wishes to be wholly

[1] Omer Englebert, *The Lives of the Saints* (New York, Barnes and Noble, 1994), 339.

forgotten were not realized after all—else how could we be given that life as example? Had her most ardent wish been granted, we would be the less for the loss both to the Church and to the world.

Today the Catholic Church, quite justly, is seen as a *sign of contradiction* in the midst of the history that unfolds around us. At a time when most other institutions and cultures seem swept up in the evils and follies of the day, the Church must often appear to stand virtually alone as naysayer, by herself holding fast to those principles and truths she proclaims shall never change though all else about her is altered or transformed.

The Church has become, almost by default, the true counterculture throughout a world fast descending into a new barbarism, a dehumanized world gathered round the altar of materialism. Of course, for the Church, her Founder began it all, this turning of all our fondest notions upside-down, when He taught the crowds by His sermon on the mount. Nothing has been altogether the same since, though man has learned little from what was said there.

The "success" to be gained in the world's eyes, the principal goal of most, wherever one looks, has assumed a high level of respectability. It is in fact granted the status of a virtue in the industrialized world. Those who attain it are said to count, to possess the greatest worth. They are made pillars of the community, to be given the place of honor. They are to be listened to when they speak, admired as they pass. They are the visible manifestation of what the rest of society most desires.

To be so visible, in the public eye, to have one's name on everyone's lips—this is the end-all, the true measure of a person's life, of whether it has been well or badly spent. Should one not attain so prized a goal, he has not become what he can be, what either God or man intended he be. He lacks true excellence, is without real honor, shall soon be forgotten, and shall die unknown.

Nothing is heard throughout the land of those words that seem to have grown fainter with time: *The last shall be first, and the first last.* They are still to be found, but one must look beyond the clamor, the crowds. The words have been, in at least one case, rewritten, inscribed on stone, over the wall of a remote and darkened cave in a place far from the main centers of the world:

"I, Rosalia . . ."

THE HALLOWED EARTH

Isidore the Farmer

THEY can tell you who he was, in the villages of the mountains and valleys of northern New Mexico. They know him there as San Ysidro Labrador, a name for them as familiar as that of any more universally popularized saint whose feast is everywhere celebrated.

To the larger world outside he is, if known at all, Isidore the Farmer, scarcely a household name in the teeming cities, the technological centers of today, where land is judged for its commercial value, for what profit it shall gain for its owner in the marketplace. It is a world that cannot see the sky for its high-rise towers or spires, the monuments built to itself, or find a plot of grass beyond the confines of its crowded malls, its endless highways, its succession of industrial parks.

It is the world we were years ago warned about by Georges Bernanos:

> Hasn't the time come for us to wonder if all of our misfortunes don't have one common cause, if this form of civilization which we call industrial civilization is not an accident, a sort of pathological phenomenon in the history of humanity?
>
> One might say that it is not machine civilization so much as it is the invasion of civilization by machines, the most

serious consequence of which is to modify profoundly not merely the environment in which man lives but man himself.[1]

But people know of Isidore the Farmer where there is still land beneath their feet, where the air is yet clear, the sky may be seen, and saints such as he are better known than film stars. These New World heirs of San Ysidro are farmers themselves or, at the least, rural folk, village dwellers, the descendants of the Hispanic settlers who before them occupied this land. Their roots grow deep here, into the very soil of this place. But they have inherited more than the land. For they know in their blood how to pray, and to pray to the saints as intercessors, to those same Catholic saints whose likenesses, as *retablos*, or *bultos*—figures in the round—adorn their homes or are hung on their walls.

There with the rest can be seen the likeness of San Ysidro Labrador of twelfth-century Spain. And it is to this saint, as intercessor, they pray each spring, on May 15, his feast day, for a bountiful growing season. Their prayers do not rise to the "city saints" or theologian-saints, but to this simple man of the soil, who knew, as they do, seed and plow, hard work and patience, sun and rain.

In their true wisdom they share even more a common knowledge with their patron saint. They understand, with Saint Isidore, what the highly cultured of today have all but forgotten: that a seed must fall into the ground and die to bear much fruit. That the same seed cannot take root in rocky soil. That by the sweat of his brow is man to live.

This is, as should be plain to all, biblical wisdom, that is to say, eternal wisdom. It is true for today, as at any time. But it is a wisdom lost or forgot in the babble of our urban culture,

[1] Georges Bernanos, *The Last Essays of Georges Bernanos*, translated by Joan and Barry Ulanov (Chicago, Henry Regnery, 1955), 82.

the clamor from off the street, the roars heard from the crowd in its sporting arenas. It is within the villages of northern New Mexico and their like that such wisdom is still known.

It is of small wonder, then, that Saint Isidore was in 1947 proclaimed the patron of the Catholic National Rural Life Conference. He is a saint uniquely qualified to represent those whose simple lives are bound to both Church and land, who yet see as a gift from God the natural creation all about them, for whom labor is prayer and the seasons a recurring unfolding of His mystery.

The agrarian faith practiced here, which so unites creation to a Creator, has on occasion been expressed elsewhere than in these out-of-the-way rural hamlets. Support has come from within the highest echelons of the Catholic Church, from within the walls of the Vatican itself. If the language from Rome is more formal than that heard in furrow or field, it says in essence what could be heard on any village corner.

Pope Pius XII wrote: "We must recognize that one of the causes of the disequilibrium and confusion of world economy, affecting civilization and culture, is undoubtedly the distaste and even contempt shown for rural life with its numerous and essential activities." The Pontiff then sounded a warning for the modern age, in much the same manner as Bernanos: "But does not history, especially in the case of the fall of the Roman Empire, teach us to see in this a warning symptom of the decline of civilization?"

The saint himself has left us no such declaration or reflection on man as caretaker of the earth, as cultivator and grower, as harvester of what he may believe to be God's bounty. He did not record those thoughts which a believing man of the soil may have while working alone in the great outdoors, under the open sky, about himself and the creation that surrounds him. We have, then, but his example, in place of words. He is to be numbered among those saints whose lives must speak for themselves. There should be little to surprise us in this. He was not, after all, a man of letters. His life was the common life of men. He was San Ysidro Labrador.

Born in 1070 in Madrid, Spain, he early on went to work, as his family was poor. He became a farm laborer on the large estate of a wealthy landowner outside the city.

And there you have, in sum, about all that can be said: the life of this saint recounted in a sentence or two. For it was there, in that one place, that he was to remain for the rest of his life, engaged in what we have learned to call, most often disparagingly, menial labor, the work performed by those least skilled, the "least worthy" among us, the worst paid, those who perhaps work the longest hours. In this case it was the labor carried on by a hired hand on land he did not own.

He married, and if his daily life, his round of work, was ordinary, his wife was not. Maria Torribia is also venerated as a saint. The holy couple had one son, who died young, after which man and wife both gave themselves entirely to God.

The simple facts having to do with the life of Isidore are thus quickly and easily recorded. He was a farmhand, true, whose work years were ended where they had begun. But he was nonetheless no common farmhand, one of a crowd, indiscernible from those of his kind.

Before beginning his labors each day, he attended Mass, waking early to go to the church. But his devotions did not end there, where others might think their duties fulfilled: leading to the separation of one's secular life from the sacred. Isidore continued in prayer while working in the fields throughout the day, communing with God and, so we are assured, his guardian angels and the saints. The air he breathed while he worked in the open was sacred air, too, along with that inside the church. The soil he plowed was hallowed ground.

A hired hand such as he, even in medieval Spain, was not to be wholly unobserved. Legends about him grew. It was reported that if Isidore was late to work after he attended Mass, angels plowed the field in his stead. The rest that can be told of his life, however, is not drawn from legend. It is the very stuff of sainthood.

Though he remained a poor man to the end of his life—he was engaged in menial labor, after all—he nevertheless shared his meager provisions with those even more in need. And, like Saint Francis of Assisi, a fellow poor man of God, Saint Isidore had a love of animals, for whom he set out food in winter and in time of drought.

Saint Isidore died on May 15, 1130, and was canonized some five hundred years later in 1622. There is a daily prayer offered on his feast day that may best distill for us what we can for our benefit learn from this simply husbandman's story: "Through the intercession of Saint Isidore, the holy Farmer, grant that we may overcome all feelings of pride. May we always serve you with that humility which pleases you, through his merits and example."

In this brief prayer is found the word that, doubtless more than any other, has throughout two thousand years marked a primary distinction between the saint and the common man. This word is *pride*. To be sure, there are more than a few virtues. But none is more common to those sanctified by the Church than humility. It is a virtue possessed not only by those saints of a low worldly estate but also by those who occupied the thrones of a kingdom and by the greatest of the scholar-saints.

It is the agrarian saint who can provide a special insight into this virtue by the very nature of his daily occupation. It is from the round of his daily life that he must draw at least a portion of his humility and shed the worst of his natural pride. The plowman, the planter, and the grower, the one who harvests and works each day, not inside the walls of some structure built by the hands of man, but rather without those walls: his "workplace" is one that man has the power neither to design nor to construct but only to use, as favor or gift. He is both laborer and guest in this place, and he despoils it at his peril. Who should not feel himself humbled, and not soon lose his pride, when his productive hours are to be spent in the midst of such a creation? It is a creation the city dweller will probably witness only on infrequent excursions into the countryside and then possibly hurry through in his modern haste to arrive somewhere else, perhaps in another city little different from the one he has left.

Today he will most often fly over that ground and see nothing of it as it passes so far beneath him. It is, all of it, a patchwork, a distant sight no nearer for him than the stars at night. Nor, perhaps, does he see the stars at all, for the city lights that after dark fill his sky.

The city dweller is surrounded, even surfeited, by what human hands and minds have constructed, devised, or over time invented. Then should anyone wonder why he may come to glorify, not God as Creator, but man the builder, the maker and mover? And as *he* is one of so noble a race, that he should not glorify himself as well?

This is pride that is breathed in with the very air of the city. The dweller there has no chance to be humble, as has the countryman, who lives his every day in the presence of what man could never have created, whose mysterious ways are even beyond his poor powers to grasp fully.

It would appear not wholly by happenstance that the Enlightenment and the urbanization-industrialization of the world emerged virtually together within the span of these last centuries, when man lost both his faith and his true place in the natural creation.

But there is a temptation lurking in a return to nature, one that has again come forth from the shadows. It is a temptation not succumbed to by Saint Isidore, who, it will be remembered, continued in prayer throughout the day as he labored in the field, a creature who knew of his Creator. Nonetheless, it is a temptation that has seduced many in this present age who, in their newly found emptiness, their rebellion against all that is modern in modern life, have discovered an earlier pagan god—or, indeed, goddess—to whom they can bend the knee, as they will not do to God the Father or God the Son. That deified presence to which they have turned is the creation, not the Creator. It is, then, not God the Father but Mother Earth. Rather than shun the creation around them, as do those who are more modern, they choose instead to make of it what is worthy of their homage or worship.

So it is we have come full circle from a long ago, even ancient, time, past the likes of Saint Isidore, who prayed to the Creator of the earth to which he set his plow, past the despoilers of that earth, to those of a New Age who revere it—the same earth—as uncreated Mother, sacred in her own right for her beauty or for sustaining us.

The goddess is thus among us once more. Her siren song is heard through the land, bewitching us to return to another day that was without sin or guilt as we now know it, to a time when man was only a part of field or forest, a child of the earth from which he had sprung with the beasts of the mountains, the valleys, and the woods.

To the new breed of pagans the awe felt by the holy plow-man was woefully misdirected. Such an experience of awe for the modern man is to be refocused from what is above him to what is around him and beneath his feet, away from what is greater than he and toward that clay from which he has been formed.

The holy plowman knew true humility, and his kind shall yet inherit the earth—if not the earth, then the Kingdom to come. Men know of Saint Isidore where it matters, where the land has not been corrupted, where their prayers for a bountiful harvest still rise to San Ysidro Labrador.

THE JOYFUL MARTYR

Théophane Vénard

THE martyrs are judged to be either profoundly courageous or outrageously foolish, depending upon one's view of the world, of man, and of revelation. But none can say that they were indifferent, that they were lacking in fervor. It is the one charge that cannot be laid against them in the two thousand years since their Master, who prefigured their kind, set by His own free act the standard each in his own way was to follow.

It was without question the highest standard. Even the most faithful, who so venerate the martyrs of the Church, find it difficult to fathom fully the price those martyrs have paid, not merely in giving up their very lives, but in the suffering beforehand they were often forced to endure. Theirs was, after all, the supreme wager. They would be granted no second chance, should it happen that their faith was without foundation and the promises made by Christ only fictions created by the Evangelists for some reasons of their own.

Though we venerate them, we remain unsure of ourselves in the presence of the martyrs, doubtful that we could withstand so much as a small part of what they were forced to endure. Should we put ourselves in their place, we find ourselves wanting. They are, we have come to agree, a breed unto themselves, even as we may still wonder where the Church and the Gospel she preaches would be today were it not for the blood shed by those we cannot imitate in deed. Were it not that they were more courageous, greater "fools", than we.

Despite such a price paid, the roster of martyrs is a long one. Its sheer length best speaks to the Truth they preached to their last breath. The supreme sacrifice of none, then, is to be thought unique: the single martyr—to the good fortune of the Church—is but one of a sizeable crowd! In this sense his blood is but a drop in a great pool, a pool added to through the ages to this day.

Then what is there to be said for one such martyr, Saint Théophane Vénard, that could be thought sufficient reason for special veneration? It would be that he can in truth be called the *joyful* martyr, so intent was he upon giving up his life for Christ. Martyrdom became his one goal in life, a life that might have been most joyless indeed had he not been granted his more ardent desire, not only to die, but to suffer, too, in imitation of his Lord.

This is in no sense to say that there have not been other martyr-saints who did not willfully, yes, even gladly, lay down their lives for the faith, and with astonishing grace. Early in the history of the Church there was Saint Ignatius of Antioch, who while in chains and on his way to Rome to be exposed to the wild beasts wrote to his followers: "May I become agreeable bread to the Lord." Or again, as is oft repeated, there was the heralded English martyr Saint Thomas More, who expressed his wish to the judges who condemned him that "we may yet hereafter in heaven merrily all meet together to our everlasting salvation."

Perhaps it is but a matter of degree, yet some difference is clear. These two great saints and their like, once they found martyrdom was to be their fate, accepted that fate with a boundless courage, all but serenely. Saint Théophane Vénard, for his part, from his youth longed for the martyr's crown, and from his earliest days he set forth to seek it out.

Théophane Vénard was born in a small French town, Saint-Loup-sur-Thouet, on November 21, 1829. He was pious from childhood and a member of a religious and remarkably tight-knit family that included a sister and two brothers. This closeness of the family members—he was especially fond of his sister, Melanie—makes much more telling, even poignant, his desire, while still a youth, to follow the path he believed to be laid out for him.

For Théophane already foresaw what he wished to make his destiny, and later, when he was to prepare himself for further vocational training to enter the priesthood, he significantly chose to enroll in the Foreign Mission Seminary for East Asia, which was located in Paris. This seminary was in all respects a training ground for would-be martyrs to be sent to a part of the world that was largely hostile. There was, in fact, in the mission house of the seminary, a Hall of Martyrs in which were displayed the relics of some who had died in the East for the faith, the instruments of torture used upon them, and pictures of their martyrdom.

His family, as would be expected, was saddened by the life he had chosen; aware of his deeply felt wishes, however, they gave their consent. Théophane, always cheerful, wrote them letters filled with affection. He faced his future as one preparing for any life's work and attempted to keep up his family's spirits. He wrote them at one point, "A cross is given us. Let us embrace it generously, and thank Him." He wrote again, echoing the words of Saint Thomas More: "We shall meet one another in heaven."

Wishing to leave little to chance, he asked to be assigned to the Tonkin mission, in what is today Vietnam. This mission was, as he said, the most to be desired, for it promised almost certain martyrdom. Once he was ordained a priest, he soon sailed for Asia. While en route there, as if with full knowledge of his future, he wrote to request of his family, "Pray for those among whom I am going to work . . . for whom I would gladly give my life."

Théophane learned the Chinese language in Singapore and Hong Kong as he waited to continue on to the mission field. Then it was on to Tonkin, with the words of his bishop to reflect upon. The bishop had counseled him not to be "an apostle by halves". The bishop need not have feared! This was scarcely a reluctant apostle whom he had so exhorted. The new missioner wrote to a priest friend, "Every time the thought of martyrdom comes across me, I thrill with joy and hope." For the three great objects of his life, he confessed, were work, the salvation of souls, and death.

He was not destined to be frustrated in his pursuit of any of those ends. In this land where he was to work saving souls, his life proved to be, as was expected, in constant peril. It was a land in turmoil and ferment, often fiercely anti-Christian, highly suspicious of foreigners, and largely under the control of mandarins, many of whom were by any standards cruel, even sadistic, and most proficient in the vilest forms of torture. Those mandarins saw the Christians as engaged in treason and rebellion against the state, and they had sworn to stamp out this alien faith at any cost. At the least, they made a practice of forcing Christians, or those they suspected of being Christians, to trample on the cross or to face certain torture or death.

As if it could not have been otherwise, with the "joyful martyr" now on hand, the persecution only intensified during those years when Théophane Vénard worked and evangelized in Tonkin. He and his fellow priests made their rounds in secret, never for one moment out of danger, offering the sacraments to those of this troubled and bloodied land who were brave enough to embrace the faith and courageous enough to face, with the priests, the ever-present prospect of a cruel scourging and death for the beliefs they held. Their churches, schools, and homes were often burned to the ground at the same moment when they were suffering the greatest physical torment.

For Théophane, there was the added burden of his poor health. He had never been truly robust, and the conditions under which he was now compelled to live were, to say the least, not those that would permit him to think much whatever of his bodily well-being. He seemed always ill and more than once feared he would die of his sickness. It was not death he feared, as should by now be entirely clear, but only that he would die "in his bed" and so be robbed of the true martyr's death for which he longed. Though his life was each time spared—"my hour has not yet come", he wrote to his family—the daily existence he endured was a kind of death in itself. The fact that, because of the peril he faced every hour, many times he could not give the sacraments or say Mass meant for him that he was to "follow the way of the Cross". He was victim even of unknown sorrows. In 1859 his beloved father died, but word of his death never reached Théophane.

His was a daily brush with death. The letters he somehow managed to write, under the worst duress, were nonetheless joyful, even though one mandarin or another seemed always to be in the area in force with his troops, scavenging for the priest and his fellow Christians. Théophane hid in boats on a river, in caves, in the homes of those bold enough to conceal him.

In 1860, while he made his base within the walls of a convent, he was confined for days on end inside a small, dark hole with, as he reported, spiders and rats and toads, during a time when outside those walls the search for him went relentlessly on. He believed he was in God's good time to face an especially inhuman form of torture and subsequent death. The mandarins had refined the tortures they inflicted upon their victims to a degree hardly matched elsewhere in the annals of fallen man.

To cite but a shortened list:

There was the "cangue", a ladder-like device, weighing up to forty pounds, which was placed over the prisoner's shoulders and which he bore about day and night till his shoulders were rubbed raw and the pain was all but unbearable.

Then there were the stocks, in which his feet were secured, the wood biting as a vise into the flesh of his ankles, so he was not able to move from a sitting or crouching position.

The knout, or whip, was used for flagellation, the torment many times lasting for several hours. After this might come the pincers, sometimes red hot, which tore the martyr's flesh from his body while he was bound to the ground.

Should he refuse to trample upon the cross, as commanded, he might be forced to kneel on a piece of wood driven through with nails so that the nails pierced his flesh down to the bone.

These, then, were the sorts of torments to which the joyful martyr had chosen to expose himself when he day after day sought out the unbaptized or offered the sacraments to the faithful. His days of service, as he well knew, were by their very nature numbered, and in 1860, betrayed by a pagan, he was at last found and seized. And what did he have to say of this, his woeful fate? "God in his mercy has permitted me to fall into the hands of the wicked", he wrote home. Then this: "Adieu, my loved ones, till our meeting in heaven."

The much sought-after captive was placed in a bamboo cage, much as any beast of the jungle, with a chain round his feet and his neck. It was a chain, he said, "which binds me to Jesus and Mary". His spirit was not only *not* broken by such ill treatment, he was, to the contrary, buoyed up, his assurance bolstered, so much so that he instructed the curious, the visitors to his cage, in the faith!

He was in time taken to Kecho, the capital, where he was to appear before a judge. Here began an odd waiting period, a bizarre deathwatch of a kind, when he was on occasion let out of his cage. But, confined or not, he visited with those who, for whatever purpose, crowded about him.

There were surprises as well. "The great mandarin has twice invited me to dinner", he was to report. His bishop recorded of him: "He is as merry in his cage as a little bird."

Still, true to his character, he looked forward to the day of his execution and expressed disappointment when time passed and his summons failed to arrive, saying, "When my head falls under the ax of the executioner, receive it, O loving Jesus!"

The summons for which he so longed came at last, and his cage was borne by eight soldiers to the place where the judge of criminal cases sat. There Théophane addressed the questions put to him with such wisdom and such grace, it was as if his words came from the mouth of the first martyr, Saint Stephen, when he stood before those who condemned him.

Commanded to trample the cross underfoot, Théophane of course refused. "Heaven having permitted my arrest," he told the mandarin, "I have confidence in God that He will give me sufficient courage to suffer all torture and be constant in death."

He surely had that courage, though he was but thirty-one years of age. He faced all with a remarkable demeanor, despite the fact that the sequence of events that led up to his execution and his execution itself were filled with horrors.

Viaticum was brought him, but it was taken away by the suspicious soldiers. The saint, unlike himself, cried out at this, not for his loss only but for fear that the Body of Christ would be profaned. And before a Host could reach him a second time, Théophane had been led off to meet his executioner.

This man without question seemed cast for a black role in a horror film. He is described as a monstrous hunchback who had once served as a soldier but was now considered little more than a buffoon. He had put other priests to death, and he had asked to execute Father Vénard, as he coveted the clothing of the condemned man. Théophane had prepared himself for what he considered this sacred rite of his anointing with a cotton garment, which he wore beneath a long robe of black silk.

The grisly headsman, not wishing to soil with blood so fine a prize for himself, thought to strike a bargain with his victim. He asked of the saint what he would give him for a quick, clean stroke of the sword. The reply that came cannot fail to astound even one by now aware of the sanctity and devotion of Théophane Vénard—and his lifelong desire to suffer, at last, the same cruel fate as his Master. "The longer it lasts," he answered, "the better it will be!" After so startling a response, he was made to remove all his clothing save for his trousers, so that his humiliation would be complete. This was to be no less than his own Golgotha, his longed-for imitation of Christ.

The execution took place on February 2, 1861. At the hands of the merciless hunchback who wielded the sword, it was indeed a barbarous affair. The first blow barely entered the flesh, a second did not completely sever the head. Then a hacking with the sword began, so offensive it drew angry murmurs from the crowd, before the executioner-sadist held up the head for his superiors to see.

Sympathizers within the crowd rushed forward to soak their papers or whatever they had in the martyr's blood. The head was to be exposed for three days, but the saint's followers, by a ruse, gained possession and threw it into the river. However, they attached it to a line so that later they could safely retrieve it from the water. Théophane's relics, including the chain he wore that he said "binds me to Jesus and Mary", were over time distributed far and wide, to his family and followers and to others—to the same Hall of Martyrs at the Foreign Mission Seminary in Paris where young Théophane himself had once venerated the relics of those priests who had gone before him to gain the martyr's palm.

How fitting that one of the relics found its way to the Carmelite cloister of the Little Flower of Jesus, Saint Thérèse of Lisieux, whose devotion to Saint Théophane Vénard has been attested. This was the same Thérèse who had written that she wished "to spend my heaven doing good on earth" and who was later to be named by Pope Pius XI as patron saint of Catholic missions.

The story of Théophane Vénard, its closing chapter in any case, may be too grotesque a tale to please some. It offends our modern-day sensibilities, even in an age of such gross random violence. The elements it possesses of the bizarre, the sheer horror of those last moments as they relentlessly unfold, seem to make it less a story of one man's towering sanctity than a macabre tale.

Still, it is not the fearsome human depravity on display here that alone unsettles. Modern man has to a degree grown used to the savage within himself, the brutish behavior we see all about us that erupts through the thin veneer of a world that believes itself thoroughly civilized.

Pope John Paul II called the twentieth century the "age of martyrs", when the world endured the twin scourges of Nazism and Communism, to name but two of the man-made plagues the earth has experienced and, in one sense or another, survived. Martyrs we have had of late, and these latter-day martyrs have often suffered and died under circumstances as grueling as those undergone by Saint Théophane Vénard.

However, there is something more in the life and death of Théophane that must amaze and astonish, an added dimension we can barely imagine and only dimly comprehend— something that goes beyond the diabolic character of his execution. It is the clear *eagerness* with which he met his cruel fate, the gladsome spirit with which he sacrificed his life. For it is one thing to die humbly, with a quiet dignity and true faith, for the Gospel. Therein lies a full sanctity, too. It is another to seek out, zealously and joyfully, such a bloody destiny as this—in fact, to center one's entire life upon the achievement of just such a fate.

In this regard even the contemporaries of Théophane Vénard, those who knew him best and to the last, were moved by his fervor, by what he was. One, a Bishop Theurel, wrote to his family after the saint's death: "His confidence in God was boundless, and made him bold almost to a fault. . . ."

To a fault? There, expressed in but three words, is summed up what we observe, in our own confessed weakness, in the presence of such a man as this. In the light of such confidence as he revealed, we fall back at what we cannot fully grasp.

The saint himself has given us a sense of that spirit with which he was so richly endowed in this thought, which he left for our reflection: "We are all flowers planted on this earth, which God plucks in His own good time, some a little sooner, some a little later."

THE MARTYR OF MOTHERHOOD

Margaret Clitherow

T HE woman at hand, the wife of one John Clitherow, was the mother of three. Therein is the crux of the matter, the true heart of her story, in so plain and ordinary a circumstance as this. Nothing else about her would, in an age more virtuous than ours, so define her, so spell out what she offered upon the altar of her belief, in full trust that her sacrifice came from the deepest love for those she had brought into the world.

When this Elizabethan Age mother was at times forced to leave her children, as happened on more than one occasion, it was not so she might go to office or workplace, to some social affair where she might further herself in some manner. It was not so she could in some way enhance her place in life and thus heighten her self-esteem. Rather, Margaret Clitherow went off to jail. At the last, she was to endure a most painful death.

If she is today to be given her full due, one has first to agree to a basic premise that is scarcely allowed in modern feminist thought. This is to say that the bond between mother and child has no equal, in human terms, among all creatures of the earth. It is to assert that the one who bears the infant within her own body is destined by nature itself to be the most closely joined to the child that is born—whatever her wishes in the case—by a bond that is lasting and final.

Thus it is foremost in her role as mother that we want to observe Margaret Clitherow. Only in so doing can we offer proper homage to the martyr. The gift of her own life is otherwise somehow diminished.

We must first come upon her, though, as young Margaret Middleton, born around 1553 in England, in the northern part of the country. This era of great religious strife, involving the persecution of Catholics—the same conflict that would later cost her her life—appeared not to have affected her in the least in her early years. She is pictured as pretty, even vivacious, and merry, the popular daughter of Protestant parents.

In 1571 she was married to a widower, John Clitherow, a butcher by trade and a man with his eye on political appointment. It is worthy of note, in light of what is to follow, that she was in these unsettled times considered to be a "safe" bride for such a tradesman and member of the community, as she seemed interested only in the enjoyment of things.

This calls for a word on John Clitherow himself, for his was not to be a minor role in the drama that ensued. But if his was a principal part, it was also, sadly, that of the weakling in the plot: a sympathetic character for the tastes of some, perhaps, but much too timorous for the rest.

Clitherow was the cautious man of business found in every generation, the sort to risk nothing for an unpopular, or proscribed, cause. If he indeed preferred, as was said, the Catholic Church then outlawed by Queen Elizabeth, he nevertheless wished to carry about him no scent of controversy, particularly in those later years when he sought appointment or election to local public office in York, where the couple lived.

He dutifully went, then, to the state church so as to avoid being branded a "papist" or "schismatic", charges that could have cost him business and, as religious tensions heightened, even land him in prison. It was no small matter of concern for him, then, when, three years after his seemingly "safe" marriage, his attractive and spirited young wife became a Catholic.

The reasons behind her conversion are somewhat obscure, though it is pointed out that her generation still had memory of the Catholic Church as she was before she was ruled illegal and her faithful and priests driven underground by edict of the queen. There is some hint, however, of young Margaret's thinking in a statement reported by Father John Mush, her confessor and source of much that is known about her life. She was baptized, she said, after "finding no substance, truth nor Christian comfort in the ministries of the new gospel, nor in their doctrine itself, and hearing also many priests and lay people to suffer for the defense of the ancient Catholic faith".

The faith she now professed she did not take lightly. It was in time to become the very substance of her being. From prison she was later to write that "I mean to live and die in the same Faith; for if an angel come from heaven, and preach any other doctrine than we have received, the Apostle biddeth us not to believe him."

The stage then was set for a morality play of the highest order, when such sentiments as these were expressed within a society whose government each year grew more repressive for those Catholics who remained in its midst. There was surely pathos enough here, for Margaret was to the end a dutiful wife who loved her husband, as she confessed, "next to God in this world".

Next to God, she declared. Then there was sure to be conflict, only waiting its moment. She proceeded to harbor priests, by now a capital offense, so that Mass could be said in her home. Additional damning evidence against her could be found in her cupboards and closet: holy pictures, the vessels, chalices, vestments, and altar bread needed for Mass. All of this, she well knew, not only endangered herself but the life— and, of course, the business—of her husband, who was by then prospering in his trade.

There was soon even more to be considered. For there were the couple's three children to think of. The Clitherows had two sons and a daughter, who, in order of birth, were named Henry, Anne, and William. The "martyr of motherhood" here took on flesh, emerging from inside the walls of an ordinary tradesman's home. Margaret was a woman of strong affections, whose family was the center of her life. While strict with her children, she loved them with the most heartfelt devotion. It was in this very love for her own that her real martyrdom was to grow, in the full surrender of those so dear to her to the care, the safekeeping, of God.

She would not only put their daily lives at risk by having her children schooled in the Catholic faith at home. She was off and on during this period forced to be parted from them when she was taken to jail, where she was one time confined for two full years. It is, in fact, unclear whether or not her youngest child, William, was born to her while she was behind bars.

So mindful and caring as she was, she could not but have been wholly aware of how, in her very concern for both the lives and the souls of her children, she was making them outcasts from the world they saw all around them. This world was also the world of their father, whom Margaret, to her great sadness, failed ever to convert, even with her death at the hands of the state.

When she was on those occasions arrested, her children were taken into custody, too, as the authorities attempted to force them to attend a state church. She could then do no other, as mother, than surrender them in full trust to the providence of God, to abandon them in the way she had abandoned herself. She would say this was so to the last. She would maintain she loved her children so deeply she would rather they, despite their tender years, endure such tribulation than that they, through any show of weakness on her part, should fall into heresy when it came to the faith.

This was to be made abundantly clear when, brought to trial, she responded to her judges, who sought to dissuade her from her beliefs by asking her to consider the welfare of her family. She informed them forthrightly: "I would to God my husband and children might suffer with me for so good a cause."

The judges, as might be imagined, took this as a sign of an appalling hardness on her part, that she wished those she most loved be put to death with her. She of course meant no such thing. The truth was she but wanted for them the same constancy of faith as she was now privileged to make visible. This, then, was true mother love, as she saw it, a love her all-too-human judges failed to distinguish or understand in the saintly woman who stood before them.

The life of Margaret Clitherow could have had, in the age through which she lived, but a single ending, one that might have been foretold. No other closing scene could have been written for one who proved herself to be so dauntless in living out all she believed, however high the price she was made to pay.

Like Ralph Milner, another English martyr of her time, Margaret, when not in jail, appeared to be courting arrest. When possible, she began each day with a Mass in her home. If no priest, whom she might secretly harbor, was on hand, she spent that hour or two of the morning in prayer.

But she was wont to be found in a more open display of her faith when she was outside the confines of her home. In the area where she lived was a gallows where the bodies of the martyrs who had gone before her were sometimes left hanging for days. This somber and bloodied place of execution had been turned into a ready-made shrine by those brave souls yet willing to display their adherence to the teaching of the Church of Rome.

It was here Margaret Clitherow could often be seen at prayer—here where so much blood had been shed, where she must surely have sensed that the shadow of the same gallows fell across her where she knelt on the ground.

And so the inevitable happened. She was arrested a last time in 1586, at which time the authorities broke into her home to find the Catholic school in full session. One boy in the class broke down under questioning to reveal where the Mass vestments and altar furnishings were to be found hidden away.

Two of her children, Anne and William, were given into the care of Protestants. Then it was discovered that the oldest, Henry, had been sent abroad to attend Catholic school there, an act that was in defiance of the law as well.

Margaret was not to see her children again. Still she would not yield, and she was hauled before the council of judges. Here began her true passion.

Though she was not allowed visits from her children, it would seem that any others might come to her cell if they wished to try to weaken her resolution—or if they had been sent for that purpose. Friends came who tried to dissuade her. Protestant ministers were dispatched to see her, to argue theology with the woman they knew to be unlettered but whom they found to be filled with a simple wisdom that would never allow her to be shaken.

The torture she was compelled to endure was often subtle, though nonetheless terribly real. She was accused, in for her the cruelest of all slanders, of having had affairs with the priests she had brought into her home. Even this base calumny she bore heroically. She placed her faith in the truth and would not be swayed.

Never, she said, would she plead guilty to treason, with which she was charged, for how was it then treasonable to hold fast to the true faith? Nor would she agree to have her case placed before a jury, which was more likely to acquit her. For if she were to do so her children would be forced to testify, and as a devoted mother she did not want this to occur.

She reasoned as follows: If the children lied about her state-proscribed activities in order to save her, they would be guilty of sin. But again, should they tell the truth and afterward she were sentenced to death, they might then feel that the guilt for her fate lay upon them, a guilt they might harbor within themselves for the remainder of their lives.

So it was she refused to be heard by a jury. And so it happened that the sentence meted out to her was swift and sure, a sentence extreme in its brutality. A judge named Clinch rendered the judgment upon her:

> You must return from whence you came, and there, in the lowest part of the prison, be stripped naked, laid down, your back upon the ground, and as much weight laid upon you as you are able to bear, and so to continue for three days without meat or drink, except a little barley bread and water, and the

third day to be pressed to death, your hands and feet tied to posts, and a sharp stone under your back.

In short, she was to be crushed till she breathed her last.

It is testimony to the character of Margaret Clitherow that while it was with great dignity and calm that she heard this merciless sentence pronounced upon her—she was, after all, to suffer and die for her faith—yet she was greatly disturbed that she was to be stripped naked for that sentence to be carried out. She spent a part of the few days left her making herself a garment, one properly fitted for the carrying out of her sentence, but full enough to cover her body too.

Through these last days she fasted. She was, however, seldom alone, for the regular band of ministers continued to appear in a final effort to "save" her, both from her executioners and from her faith.

They, of course, failed, and the hours passed. She was not without the most human of passions. At times she was found to be cheerful. Then she grew fearful. She was young, and much too vibrant, to die! There were the children for her to think of, whose futures she could only consign to God.

To a friend she confided, "The sheriffs have said that I am going to die this coming Friday; and I feel the weakness of my flesh, which is troubled at this news, but my spirit rejoices greatly. For the love of God, pray for me and ask all good people to do likewise."

She sent her headdress, which all housewives of that time wore, to her husband as a sign of her duty to him who was her head. To her daughter, Anne, she gave her shoes and her stockings. This was, she said, so that the young girl might follow in her footsteps.

When the fateful morning arrived, she was led out through the crowd that had formed in the street to the nearby place of execution. There she prayed for the Catholic Church, the pope, and all the clergy. And there she was ordered for a last time to confess she died for treason. To this, for a last time, she cried out it was not so. "I die for the love of my Lord Jesu." With this she lay quietly down, her hands still folded in prayer.

There is something of a mystery here. Why the three days of slow death pronounced as part of her sentence did not now follow is not clear. For a sharp stone was next placed beneath her back, then a door laid upon her as her two hands were fastened to stakes in the floor. Then four beggars hired for the job lay the weights upon the door, those weights which would, when sufficient in number, crush her to death.

The saintly woman was heard to utter at the end: "Jesu! Jesu! Jesu! have mercy on me!"

It required fifteen minutes or so for her to die.

That Margaret Clitherow might be accounted a loving mother is not easily seen. She was a woman who, in real measure, abandoned her children at the very age they were most likely to require her maternal care.

To understand fully, we must enter the mind-set of the saint. It is a mind-set into which the greatest portion of mankind seldom intrudes. This is where "our time", as we know it, is wholly altered, the concept of mere hours and days and years shattered. It is where a man's entire lifetime becomes little more than prelude to all that follows, to a grandeur beyond any poor mortal's power to portray in words.

If this be the truth of the matter, then how much lessened is the pain of the here and now, the agony of the moment, the gain or loss, even the parting from loved ones if that parting is to be but for this brief while.

For the saint the transitory world so evident around us is as a door that leads into the next room, where he hopes to find gathered, then or in the future, all those he has known and loved, so that he has only to pass through this door to join them there. It is a door that appears to be bolted fast in the eyes of the common lot of men, so belabored as they are by the ordinary round of days, the passing scene, the press of the crowd. But for the saint, with his keener sight, it is a door opened wide, so that in effect the two rooms became as one, sharing much the same light and air in order that he might feel at home in both one and the other.

So it was for Blessed Margaret Clitherow. To her mind she could act on her love for her children only by parting from them, in this world, for the cause she knew to be just and true, placing them fully under the care of God. For her to do otherwise would have been to fail in that motherly love, to place in peril their mortal souls. She wished most to provide for their joy in heaven.

If parting from them was grievous for her now, any such grief was not to be lasting but would give way to the true joy of reunion when time itself was no longer.

In her case, it is worthy of mention that something of what she had hoped and prayed for was to come to pass in the world she left behind. The unswerving faith she had revealed during those few arduous years of her ordeal was not to go unrewarded.

Though her husband never showed real courage or strength, at the end he could not help but display his true feelings. When he was informed of the condemnation of Margaret, he wept as he said bitterly, "Will they kill my wife? Let them take all I have and save her, for she is the best wife in all England, and the best Catholic also."

But it was left to her three children to attest best to the force of the example she had bequeathed to them in her life and her death. Both her sons became priests, and her daughter became a nun. Margaret Clitherow would most surely say that, with this, her work on earth as wife and mother had at last been completed, her task fulfilled.

THE MADMAN

Benedict Joseph Labre

H E is to be seen everywhere along the city's street now-adays: the madman among us. An ill-clothed derelict, he is there on the corner we pass, a man whose ravaged face we should as soon not see. The sight of him, while no longer uncommon, is still not one we can claim to have got used to.

The man is, in our wishful thinking, harmless, surely a menace to no one but himself. Yet one can never be sure. There is no such guarantee in this life, nor do the most of us want to tempt fate. The evening news is filled with stories that concern the pillagers loose throughout the land, those men, whether evil or merely sick, who prey upon women and other men and, yes, children as well, the innocent in our midst.

Then who is there to distinguish the one from the other of those we pass on the corner, who after a time appear so alike to our gaze? Who will tell the streetcorner beggar, harmless if frightening in appearance, from the true madman with theft, even murder, in his heart? How can one judge from his looks what is there, when he is hardly more than a shadow? Mother Teresa of Calcutta saw Christ in the poorest of the poor. But we have not so keen an eye.

The madman, in one guise or another, has never been missing from any age. The poor you shall always have with you. So we have been told, and among those poor who are with us, we know well, shall be the likes of the madman.

But one form of "madman" seems all too scarce in the doorway or on the street today, as if his kind were to be relegated to history and, even there, to a footnote. He is from those dark ages before we became the children of the Enlightenment and so knew better than to be fooled, to look beyond this world and its pleasures. He was there before we became so puffed up with knowledge there was no place left for his sort to appear, to display for us his particular madness.

This singular madman was in his own time shunned, too. He too dwelt in the shadows, within the margins of society. But there at least he was to be found. He was the holy man of God, the fool for Christ.

In the case at hand, there was a saint to be found beneath the outer appearance of the derelict, the badly soiled and ill-fitting clothing, the unwashed creature who would seem to have come all of a sudden from nowhere. Though he was thought not to be mad in the same sense as the others of his physical likeness, neither was he a part of the common world, its habits and customs, the manner of life that went on around him.

This figure before us was Saint Benedict Joseph Labre, and he was considered by the honorable, the upright, citizens of his day altogether mad. For how else should one describe a man of his looks, his odd way of life, one who cared nothing for the comforts of home and hearth, the pleasure of a warm meal and a soft bed, the laughter had in the company of friends? There was little about him that could be understood—the poverty he had freely chosen, his rootless wandering over the earth wholly engrossed in what others could not, or would not, see, his own eyes fixed on what was invisible to their worldly gaze.

So, when he died, it took the voices of children, the innocent of the world, to make it known who the madman truly was. They were children who then cried out for all around to hear: "The saint is dead!"

The eldest of fifteen children and the son of a shopkeeper, Benedict Joseph Labre was born in 1748 in Saint-Sulpice d'Amettes, France. The young man, however, was cut out for neither shop nor trade but early on manifested the first signs he was destined for a religious vocation. Even when still a youth he was absorbed in the Scriptures.

The silent sort, one of few words, he at eighteen years of age walked sixty miles to La Trappe to join the Trappists there. But it was not to be. For even this early he showed the unmistakable traits of the social misfit, the marks of a man ill suited to life within walls with others. He was thought eccentric. His health became poor.

Though once found wanting, he was not easily dissuaded. He next tried the Carthusians but remained only six weeks in their midst. Lastly, he sought out the Cistercians. He fared no better there.

It was only now, through such trial and error, that he came to see who he rightfully was, the pilgrim of the road he was intended to become. His ascetic vocation was only then clear to him. He was to be the wandering mendicant, the poor man of God. He had waited, and then he had seen and come to know.

So moved, he set off for Rome, living on alms along the way. This first journey of the beggar-pilgrim was not to be without its memorable occurrence, of no great moment but yet of some interest.

He was given hospitality, food, and a bed in the home of a man named Pierre Vianney. There the strange wayfarer, welcomed beneath this roof as a man of sanctity, was asked to bless his host's children, among them his son Mathieu. When he grew up, the lad then blessed was to become the father of Jean-Marie Vianney, the priest who became the fabled Curé d'Ars, the saint of the soiled and threadbare cassock, one who in his own time would be almost as poor as the onetime houseguest of his grandfather.

Once arrived in the Eternal City, Benedict Joseph Labre soon became known as "the beggar of Rome", though he was in truth still the silent man, a "beggar" who seldom opened his mouth to speak, even to ask for alms—one who, saying nothing, relied on the goodness of others. If, as happened, he were given nothing, he subsisted on those leftover or throwaway scraps of food he could find, or he did without. The saint with little has more to share than the rich man blessed with all he owns. On occasion he passed on what he was given, or the food he could find, to another he thought more needy than he.

After a stay in Rome, he resumed his life of a pilgrim on the road, setting off on foot to visit the various principal shrines of western Europe. This time he was no more than before the ordinary pilgrim, the commonplace tourist, for like the apostles, when instructed by Jesus and sent forth on their mission, he took no provisions for the way. He slept on the ground or in some roadside shed. There he might be discovered, in a frayed cloak, worn and broken shoes on his feet.

Henri Ghéon, in his admirable work *The Secret of the Curé d'Ars*, paints a striking word picture, almost as an aside, of this poor pilgrim, this fool of Christ. He was, writes Ghéon,

> the poor man *par excellence*, flung aside, jeered at, beaten— occasionally even received with kindness, which was more than he showed himself. He fasted three times a week, bore heat and cold, swarmed with vermin, prayed always and never

spoke. He replied by a nod with the greatest friendliness. He visited all the famous shrines—Rome, Loreto, Compostella—spending one half his life tramping, the other half on his knees.

It was as though the sorrowful shade of Christ walked this refined and irreligious world, to warn it of the gulf into which it was soon to fall.

Labre, this mad and homeless Christlike man, returned in time to Rome, where, for the most part, he remained after 1774. But here his life was much the same as when he had walked the country roads. He could not alter what he was. He spent his nights in the ruins of the Coliseum, his days praying inside the churches of the city.

Then, as if it were destined for him from the beginning, the clear fate for one who cared so little for his body and so much for his soul, he was forced by ill health into a hospice for destitute men, where, after all, he could be in the company of his own kind.

Those roads he had taken all surely led here, where the poor and the mad are gathered from the street, out of the sight of the men who carry out the business of the day. They are here, out from underfoot in the world of commerce with its traffic, the world of the shop, the theater, and the bazaar.

In 1783 he caught a chill and suffered from a bad cough. But he was not to be denied—he was mad, after all, and could not be kept from what his heart was set upon. And so it was that, even so ill, he was to be found at Mass.

It was Wednesday of Holy Week. Surely it was fitting that it was on a day just before the Passion that he felt faint and left the church to sit on the steps outside. He could not be taken home, as another might, to be surrounded and cared for by family, neighbors, and friends. The man had no such home. Thus it transpired that he could only be removed to a nearby

house—*the borrowed tomb*, in a striking sense, of his Master—
where he was given the last sacraments and died.

Then it was that the cries of the neighborhood children
were to be heard in the street, the first to proclaim who it was
that lay on a stranger's bed: "The saint is dead!" Their cries
indeed proved to be prophetic. Benedict Joseph Labre was
canonized one hundred years later, in 1883.

The descriptive phrase "fool for Christ" has an archaic ring,
if uttered today. For the young it may have no meaning whatever. They understand the simple words that are spoken, but
know nothing of what, or whom, they are intended to portray. For it is a concept simply beyond their experience and
the life they have, during their few short years, observed
around them.

They may have seen any number of their elders who professed themselves Christians at home, in public, or at worship.
But they have not likely witnessed any who might represent
such a fool as this, one possessed by so great a fervor to follow
the Gospel at all cost. The silent, ragged figure *there* who is
oblivious to the fact that the eyes of the curious, the amused,
or the openly hostile are turned upon him. The one said, in
whispers that go round, to be a scandal.

No. This man, chances are, the young have not seen,
though as the children of this much-traveled age they have
roamed widely and lived, as they believe, deeply. They can
boast, and with a good deal of truth, that they have seen
everything this modern culture provides. Nothing is missing
from their experience—save the one sight that might have
tempered or transfigured all the rest.

And their elders? They least of all would wish to be called a
fool. They shall more readily assent to any name but this. To
be styled as untrustworthy, unfaithful, selfish, or thoughtless,

a sinful man, even a drunk or a brute, is not in this day and age regarded as outright slander. For in a time when each man may fashion his own truth and consider one truth altogether as good as another, one can say that another's view of himself is all in the eye of the beholder.

What, then, is faithless, or sinful, or at the least distasteful to one may appear not at all so to another. The scarlet letter worn by Judy will be no more than a fashion statement for Jane.

But to be called a fool! And a fool for Christ? This is quite another matter. There is little of true or false involved here. A fool is a fool in any language. Then it is not a question of strict definition, or one's own truth, of whether one lives here or there, of a person's background or training or experience. To be thought of anywhere as a fool is to draw on oneself ridicule and scorn, to be the probable object of derisive laughter from the crowd. The strongest among us can endure all but that. We shall be feared, shunned, even hated. But to be made out to be a fool? No—never!

This particular fool, the singular madman, the fool for Christ, will doubly suffer the taunts, the catcalls, the mockery reserved for those who so disregard the ways of the world, its own ordered standards, the prevailing fashions of the crowd. He has been promised as much by Christ Himself.

But the fool will appear in our midst again, as surely as saints have been sent us in those times of the greatest need. He shall be found when the world has become too sterile, too sane, for its own good, for its very salvation.

His life will doubtless be spent within a few years, as was the brief life of Benedict Joseph Labre. Those consumed by such zeal as this have small regard for their own well-being, the demands of the body.

And so this madman, too, shall likely fall ill one day and be taken to the home of some kind stranger, to breathe his last beneath another's roof. Then again it will require the children of the town to be the first to name him who is carried along the street, when their cries are once more heard: "The saint is dead!"

THE CALL

Nicholas of Flüe

H E might best be described as the saint of paradox, for what he once was and what he later became, for the pure breadth of his life and experience. Let us then see the man, the whole of him: the family man, father of ten, who would become a hermit; the statesman called father of his country who was to end his life as a virtual recluse; the one-time respected magistrate and judge who in his later years, from the accounts of eyewitnesses, lived solely on the Eucharist, his only food.

This was, all in its turn, the life of the Swiss saint Nicholas of Flüe. It is in full measure, in its passage, an unfolding, a slow emerging of the true holy man over the period of a lifetime. There is little or none of the sudden conversion, a light from the sky, about it—nothing of Saint Paul on the road to Damascus. It is rather a matter of stages, of acts, of grace in its own good time perfecting nature.

To observe this life of Nicholas allows us not only to ponder paradox but also to weigh the role in one man's experience of those hard sayings that are to be found in the Gospels. In him we confront those words that Jesus uttered with all the force of a commandment and that we mere mortals believe to be beyond our poor powers to live by or follow, to put into practice, when we at the same time must survive in the world around us.

They are those same words, spoken as injunction, that often caused the disciples to question Him further as to their true meaning, so far did they seem beyond a man's reach, and that made others of His followers drift off into the crowd for good.

We for our part declare they were uttered with all good intention. But, beyond that, they are met with a smile. They then fall more lightly on the ear, as words surely memorable but in effect harmless: "Be perfect as your Father in Heaven is perfect. . . . Give all you have to the poor. . . . Leave the dead to bury their dead."

When we look to the life of Nicholas of Flüe, we are forced to consider this further exacting utterance of Our Lord: "If anyone comes to me and does not hate his own father and mother and wife and children and brothers and sisters, and even his own life, he cannot be my disciple."

The Scripture-wise say of this that Christ here had simply to do with a person's priorities. He hardly wished to destroy the sanctity of the family, in which He would have been the first to declare that love and faithfulness must abound.

But the words as recorded nonetheless sound harsh and much too stringent; one turns away, to look for the kinder, gentler Master: the Master found elsewhere throughout the Gospels, He of the Golden Rule, the parable of the Good Samaritan, the Shepherd caring for His sheep.

But, in the end, after all else is said, there is no evading, no denying what we have heard. There can be no quietly slipping off, taking with us only that which we wish to carry away, what we can comfortably carry, and leaving behind what is too heavy a burden for our shoulders or too great a weight for our hands. There is no escaping the knowledge that the cost of discipleship, as we have been duly warned, is high. The cost is many times to be measured against the loss of what we hold to be most dear.

Still there is this: the cost may or may not be judged high depending upon the person involved. A man without close family ties, who long ago abandoned his home and those within it and now goes his own way with no sense of either guilt or regret, would find it quite easy to boast he was a "true disciple", having left all that behind. Though his reasoning is, of course, flawed, the cost for him, in his own mind at least, is not great.

The price paid by one such as Nicholas of Flüe, however, was high indeed. There was certain loss and sacrifice. The words of Christ grated on the ear, and the call heard was final and insistent. It could no longer be answered or not answered, just as one chose. The choice had itself been taken out of one's hands. There was for him both the family in which he was reared and the one of which he was the faithful husband and father. He knew well, both as boy and man, what is meant by the familial bond.

The "ordinariness" of the first half of his life did not end there, in family ties. Through much of his adult life he was to be the conventional good citizen, the Swiss townsman performing his civic duties, hardly to be distinguished from those about him with whom he lived and worked.

He was born of pious parents in 1417 in a canton that bordered on Lake Lucerne. From the first he was in religious surroundings, within a circle known as the Friends of God, a society made up of Catholics who lived in families or small communities.

When he was twenty-two he fought as a soldier in a war with Zurich, at a time of civil strife when each Swiss canton was more an independent republic, often engaged in battle against another. That was not to be the last time he bore arms, the end of his military service. He served again, as a captain, in another such campaign fourteen years later.

Then, home once more, he was in his time a farmer, magistrate and judge, assemblyman and councilor. His private life, no less exemplary than his public service, was one of complete moral integrity. He had married Dorothy Wissling, who was also a member of the Friends of God, and the couple had ten children.

But there was another element of his life during this period that gives us real insight into the man's nature. It serves, too, as a prelude, for here we see the common public man of his day who was privately an incipient saint. We see the two lives as one, in the public chamber and inside the home, the thread of each entwined with the other. It was a son of Nicholas who was to report that his father often spent his nights praying inside his room. Or that his father, for the same purpose, frequently paid visits to a nearby church.

Nicholas' life, then, was one both of service and of true piety, one that any man might emulate: the family obligations, the work performed through each day for the common good, the hours of the night spent in prayer. It was no less than the sort of "little way" that was later to be lived out by Saint Thérèse of Lisieux.

One could rightly declare this was enough, that a lifetime so spent was the most to be asked of any man. There are saints who have done little more and still have been raised to the altars. They fashioned sanctity within the bounds of home and hearth, in everyday acts of service to others—in the routine, the common, the ready-at-hand.

But the call of God for each soul is a mystery, one beyond any sorting out by man. For Nicholas it was a singular destiny that awaited him, a call unlike that for others, a vocation that came when he was already along in years. He was fifty when he felt summoned to abandon the familiar world he knew, to leave the life he had pursued in one form or another for half a century.

Those of a questioning temperament might wonder what course such a morally incorruptible man might have chosen if at this point his faithful wife had pleaded with him, in tears, not to go but to remain with her under their roof, not to wander forth on so unsure a venture. Perhaps, when he gave it more thought he would see things differently, would see his true future more clearly, less moved by the obscure promptings of the moment.

However, such a scene did not occur. His wife played a real role in what followed, when she for her part saw beyond her own wholly human needs, beyond the most elemental desires of the heart. She did not oppose him in this matter. She, too, was a member of the Friends of God, a Catholic circle among whom a call of this sort was seen as coming from on high. That being the case, all else must give ground; no human barrier was to be raised or any obstacle placed in his path.

Thus it happened that in 1467 the erstwhile father and public figure, the respected leader in his community, set forth from his home barefoot and bareheaded, clad in a gray-brown habit, with only his rosary and a staff, much as those who were the first disciples. It was as though he had at the time not even a sure destination, no certain way he would follow, for his journey proved to be a roundabout one. The route he took turned upon itself. He was headed for Alsace. But once near there, he was warned off by Friends of God in the area. The Swiss, they informed him, were unpopular in that part of the world.

So forewarned, he returned the way he had come, a strange

pilgrim seemingly lost as to his proper or apportioned place, seeking the Holy Land. To make matters worse, he became violently ill and from that moment no longer had any desire for food or drink, a side to this saint's story that has come down to us as a mystery that transcends the reason and eludes the narrow confines of the human mind. The claim was made, and not frivolously but by firsthand observers, that in time he subsisted entirely on the Food of the Eucharist. Nothing else passed over his tongue.

But for now his journey ended in a field near his home, close to the place from which it had begun. He was found there, his only shelter a tree. He was to settle at last in a valley not far away, with a chapel and a small cell inside which he lived.

The saint's saga, even at that point odd enough to the world, might have concluded in this fashion and still be thought of as highly uncommon. How few there were like him anywhere. How many were there to say they had given up half so much as this holy man, this hermit who occupied a simple hut in the valley and who, for nineteen years, close by his onetime home and within near range of his family, lived without benefit of food or drink.

Nicholas' unusual fast was confirmed over time by no less than magistrates in the area who, honorably or not, had the hermit's cell watched for months until it was determined no one brought provisions his way.

No "provisions", that is, save the Host that sustained him. For, in due course, his friends saw to it that another chapel, this one for a priest, was erected near him so he might assist at Mass daily and communicate often.

There was sanctity to be discovered here, beyond any ordinary measure. Though it was to be found out of the way, word of it got around, as so often happens in the case of true saints. The one who, with set purpose, retreats from the world and wishes only the solitude of a far place finds the populace he has left has made its way through the desert or over the miles to come seeking at his door. In time, they came from throughout Europe to hear his counsel, searching here in this rustic hermit's abode for what it would seem they could not find at home from the most learned of their towns or cities, the trained scholars and theologians of the moment.

So began what might be called the "third life" of Nicholas of Flüe. Here the recluse and onetime public servant performed those works of charity and peace required of all Christians, civic figure and anchorite alike. It was as though the whole life of the saint had led to this hour. Though his first venture out to seek solitude had seemed a roundabout one, now it could be seen that the path he had followed throughout his entire journey was in fact a straight path with, at its end, a sure destination.

Switzerland, as has been pointed out, was at this time in the throes of internal dissension, a land torn apart by bloody civil wars. Country fought against town. Each canton was much the same as an independent republic, though they were together allied in a loose confederation. The conflict raged everywhere while the country attempted to find itself.

A peaceful solution seemed close at hand in 1481. But a troublesome, if obscure to us, point of division remained. The answer, if any could be found, was crucial to the very future of the battle-scarred nation.

The statesman sought out to resolve this particular moment of crisis, as beyond belief as it may seem, proved to be the solitary who dwelt in the hermit's cell in the valley. When there appeared to be a final impasse, a parish priest of Stans recommended the council seek the advice of the holy ascetic

Nicholas. The wise hermit was indeed consulted. He was described by one source as a figure tall, brown, and wrinkled, with thin grizzled locks and a short beard.

The compromise response brought back from the rustic's cell in the valley served the purpose and solved what had been considered an insurmountable problem. The day was saved, in so improbable a fashion as to give pause to the statesman of today, meeting in their seats of power, their advisers crowded about them in the room.

Switzerland as a united nation was thus to emerge, in a real sense, from a holy hermit's cell, from the last place one might look to find anything whatever to do with the passage of history. That holy hermit, Nicholas of Flüe, was hailed as the father of his country. He is so acclaimed today. Here is one saint who, in his own land, is venerated by Catholic and Protestant alike, and this in a country that produced such pioneer Reformation leaders as John Calvin and Huldrych Zwingli.

The saint's historic act of peacemaking was performed late in his life. He died six years later, still in his isolated cell, in 1487, and he was surrounded, it is worthy of note, by his wife and his children. His death followed a week of suffering he was said to have endured with true patience. He was canonized centuries later, in 1947.

A familiar saying is often repeated: God writes straight with crooked lines. That saying is appropriate for this saint, so God-driven that he would surrender all and set forth into the unknown, led to follow what could have seemed in the beginning for him a crooked road, a path turning on itself.

But, as happened in his case, the call comes, and though it is not a human voice that is heard, it is in its own fashion and for that reason altogether more impelling, insistent beyond any mortal command. It may summon one from what he most treasures: home and family, a lifetime of labor—the very core and substance of all that he is or wishes to be.

Then, as if it were not enough that he is asked to leave all, to make of his life what it was not, he cannot see farther than his first step. A further leap of faith is demanded from him, that he begin, though he cannot know the end, what will at the last be his true fate. He cannot, as a man with human vision, look farther than the next bend, to observe where the road might turn in either direction and lead him to where he should likely not want to go.

If he is Nicholas of Flüe, he may think himself summoned to retire from the world and soon find the world crowded round his door. He may say to himself, "I shall give these poor souls my counsel. But that is to be the last of it", and discover he is yet to be asked to resolve, in his wisdom, a question having to do with the most delicate balance between a bloody war and the blessings of peace.

The man will declare, at the end of his life, "I have got here by going round in every direction!" But the saint will know that, in God's eyes, it has all been plotted out and was perfectly clear from the start. In the eternal vision it has all been in a straight line—the shortest distance between two points.

THE CROSS

Margaret of Città-di-Castello

WE look away now, in this day and this hour of our ease and comfort. There is no purpose served, we say, in dwelling upon what is so disagreeable. There is enough that is sordid and woeful in life, and we turn our gaze from so monstrous and grisly a scene as that which even the Mother of God saw, and at firsthand, on a barren hill.

The fearful sights and sounds, the jeers, the smell of the place are missing for us, separated as we are by distance and time from the gruesome scene that came to pass on Golgotha. But still we do not care to be reminded, even in effigy, of what truly occurred there. Too real a depiction of the Crucified—the blood from side and hands and feet, the broken body, the ravaged face—offends our modern sensibilities, enough so we have cleaned Him up to make Him presentable to our eyes, acceptable for all and a stumbling block for none.

Or we have done away with the savaged and unsightly figure completely. Thus it was that Protestants long ago removed the Corpus from the plain crosses that adorn their churches, inside and out. The same plain cross has over time become so inoffensive, so proper and fitting to our tastes, it is now a favorite bit of jewelry to be worn on the ear or about the throat.

If Catholics have not gone this far, within their sanctuaries, they have not been immune to the cleansing process. The crucifix of blood and thorns, of wounded flesh and pierced side, has vanished from inside those churches that have become more refined. Or perhaps the pastor has merely wished to accentuate the less distressing, more joyful, appeal of the faith. For whatever purpose, the Risen Christ is more and more to be found, His unbloodied hands raised in the air as if in a blessing, His head untouched by any crown of thorns, His body bearing no marks of any blows. It is such a sanitized figure we often now behold, meant to edify rather than disturb. If we have gained a bit by keeping our eyes fixed on the desired goal of resurrection, we have in the process lost any real sense of the often-tortured and winding path we must follow to get there.

The wish to avoid, where possible, the unpleasant is not a new or particularly modern trait. It is, after all, only human. But still it would now appear more widespread than ever, with all the means at one's command in this day to live a life spared much discomfort. And there is the fresh interest displayed by some in Eastern religions, which promise inner release and peace, and in which one is not haunted by the spectacle of God hanging beaten and scorned between two thieves.

Yet that same God has told us of personal crosses, those crosses each one must bear despite all a man, assisted by the progress of modern science, might do to avoid them. They are quickly and easily listed: rejection by others, ill health and physical pain, the death or misery of loved ones, the shattering of fortunes, loneliness, old age. The list might go on; there would appear to be more than enough to go around.

There are those who would seem to have more than their share, their allotted portion, and who then might have some claim to speak to this generation, this age that has so sought, by any means it can find, not to suffer the outrage of human misfortune.

A unique figure of this sort at once confronts us. To reach her is possible only by way of the cross. Her name is Margaret, and she was born in Italy on the eve of the Renaissance. She is called both Margaret of Metola, after the city of her birth, in 1287, or Margaret of Città-di-Castello, for the place where she died, still a young woman, in 1320.

That there are differing accounts of the life of this saint is scarcely surprising, given her singular story and the fact that so many later sought to recount it. A twentieth-century biographer, the Dominican William N. Bonniwell, reports that "during the course of six hundred years more than twoscore writers—nearly every one of them men of unusual education—chancing upon some manuscript that contained an account of Margaret's life, thought it well worth their while to publish the story of this obscure girl."

Among these, he notes, was the great Catholic theologian Saint Robert Bellarmine, "the most erudite scholar of that time", who in 1600 conducted a thorough investigation of Margaret's life for a report he later issued.

Father Bonniwell used what he found to be those authentic portions of these documents, manuscripts, and reports to compile his book *The Life of Blessed Margaret of Castello*,[1] from whose pages the life and the times of the saint emerge.

She was born at a time of great turmoil throughout Italy, when the worst of the human condition seemed put on dis-

[1] William R. Bonniwell, *The Life of Blessed Margaret of Castello* (Rockford, Ill.: TAN Books, 1983). Original edition published under the title *The Story of Margaret of Metola* (New York: P. J. Kenedy and Sons, 1952).

play. The depths of savagery reached by the contending fac-
tions in the strife have seldom been recorded elsewhere.

Her father, one Parisio, appears cut from the same cloth as
those others who figured in the sordid history of that time.
He was a wealthy nobleman who lived in a fortress, or castle,
of Metola and was in the words of one writer "monstrously
proud, unscrupulous, and indifferent to the sufferings of others". His wife was a Lady Emilia.

The couple had been childless, with no heir to carry on
the noble line. The arrival, then, of their firstborn was quite
naturally a matter of profound anticipation. But the moment
was turned into one of the greatest despair. Their child was
not a son but a daughter. And, worse still, she appeared as all
but a monster in their midst, sent to them as a kind of cruel
joke, a merciless trick played on them by the hand of nature.
For she had not even the "mother's-eye beauty" of the newborn, beauty seen through the eye of the beholder. She was
badly deformed, dwarfed in stature, so that she would never
grow to a normal height. She was hunchbacked and destined
to be lame; her right leg was shorter than her left. Even this
was not the full extent of it, as though there were a full row of
crosses, each one to be borne by this infant in turn. The child
of the lord of the castle was blind.

There is scarcely cause, then, for surprise at the couple's
first response to this apparent calamity. Who is there to cast
the first stone? Who would dare say this was a moment for
charity? They chose to engage in deceit. They would keep
the full story secret and so let out that the newborn was not
well and unlikely to survive. In one way only did they give
ground and so much as admit their daughter was human.
Pressed by the parish priest, they reluctantly agreed to have
the infant baptized and given the name Margaret, a name chosen, it is duly reported, by the maid.

This was the entrance into life for Blessed Margaret, a phantom in her own home, an exile who dwelt in the shadows of its walls, thought of by her own as not much more than a shadow herself, banished into a corner so as not to be seen by their guests or friends.

Her full banishment was yet to come, however. Her father soon had new, diabolical plans. Since their daughter, now a young girl, was so devout a child, he said, and as she was already given over to prayer in her world of darkness, why should she not have her own chapel? Then further, why could it not be a chapel inside a neighboring church, where she might pray to her heart's content?

The deed was soon done. A small cell was built into one part of the church, the six-year-old girl was one day thrust inside, and a mason sealed up the doorway. The once furtive and phantomlike child of the castle, deformed in body and blind, was now a full prisoner, confined, it was thought, for life.

But there is no accounting for souls touched by grace. What would appear an existence so outrageous, so inhuman and bestial, as to drive one to madness failed to alter young Margaret. Those who observed her at this time called her content, even cheerful.

More than this, her sufferings, the privations she was forced to endure—she thought them not enough! This mere child— who was sightless and lame, her body shrunken, discarded by those who had given her birth, with even her once-limited freedom now taken wholly away—bound herself to a strict fast for most of the year and, not content with this, wore a hair-shirt next to her skin.

That one so young and so scourged by every sort of misfortune should be filled with so great an infusion of grace can only confound the reason. Human logic is found to be wanting when confronted with what it has no means to explain.

Margaret was held as prisoner for twelve years, sustained by the Mass, penance, and the Eucharist, all available for her inside her cell in the church that was, for all this while, her only home.

Her life was to be changed only by events taking place well outside her cell and far beyond her control. First, an invasion by hostile forces into this strife-torn area forced her parents to confine her elsewhere for a time, as they themselves fled. Then, when the threat was ended and all had returned home, they hit upon a new scheme that could, if it were successful, free them entirely from even thinking about one so unfit to look after herself as Margaret.

They had heard of miraculous cures occurring at a Franciscan shrine in the city of Castello. This was to be their salvation: a daughter whose sight was restored and her body made whole. But it was not to happen as they hoped, and we are left once more to reflect on the ways of providence. For there were, as has been said, miraculous cures reported at this shrine. Then what of Margaret? Could it be that in the eyes of God she was in need of no cure, without blemish? Could this blind and lame young woman be just as He intended she be, so there was nothing whatever He meant to have changed? Perhaps she was for the edification of us all?

The wishes of the couple from the castle were not, in any case, granted. Nothing about their daughter was altered or in any manner transformed, and they responded in a fashion wholly typical for them. They simply abandoned her in Castello. They left her, who was in their lives so great a burden, to fend for herself in the streets of a strange city.

She became what she could hardly avoid becoming, a homeless beggar who slept in doorways and drank from public fountains. And no—she was not in the least "cured" of what she had always been: instead, she was soon known throughout the city—for her cheerfulness, kindness, and patience!

It is no great surprise, then, that she was in time taken into the homes of one or another of the townsfolk, and later on she was received by the cloistered nuns of an old convent located within the gates of the city. The blind Margaret was understandably overjoyed. Now in this peaceful setting, freed from foraging each day through the streets, she might devote herself to a life of prayer.

Even here, though, she was not to be spared the weight of one more cross. Her unhappy odyssey was not yet over. The nuns, she found, largely ignored the strict Rule established for their convent. They broke the vow of silence imposed on them at certain times throughout the day. They accepted gifts from others. They entertained guests, family and friends, in the parlor.

Their newcomer, from off the streets, proved to be a problem for them. The blind young woman with her "eccentric" ways observed every letter of the Rule. She turned into a nuisance in their midst, a true thorn in the side, one for whom they could no longer feel any charity.

Her very piety was to be her undoing—this piety displayed in a convent of nuns. After a time she was, once more, out in the street.

The later years of the short life of Margaret of Città-di-Castello were, by some grace, what she might most have wished for, what for her would have seemed reward enough for her torturous journey through the years. In the church where she attended morning Mass, she met members of the Order of Penance of Saint Dominic, the Third Order Dominicans, that same order of which Saint Catherine of Siena was not long after to become a most illustrious member.

These were women who, though unable to enter a convent, wore a religious habit and followed a religious rule of life in their homes. They were older women, mostly widows, though some were married.

Margaret was, of course, young and single. She nonetheless wished to join their number with so great an ardor her desire became something of a public cause, so much so that a committee was formed to act on the matter and a report was issued on the faith and morals of the fervid blind outcast from the streets.

The result was, it is believed, historic: she was the first young, unmarried woman admitted to the Order of Penance. She could not have asked more, and her joy was unbounded. The new Dominican tertiary, clad in her habit, was vowed to the life she most wanted, one of study, penance, and prayer. Then, as if to fill to the brim her newfound cup of good fortune, she was given first one home, for a time, and later a second with well-to-do families of the city under whose roof she might follow her Rule.

From within those walls a series of miracles, of healing, were to be reported in the course of the days that followed. But the strange houseguest was not only engaged in the practice of the miraculous. She was soon to become busily involved in affairs of the world. She visited the sick and the dying and those in prison. She began a school for children.

The untutored woman, displaying something of the miraculous in her own life, too, was said to recite from memory the 150 Psalms, the Office of the Blessed Virgin, and the Office of the Holy Cross.

Margaret of Città-di-Castello had, then, by any account, come a far distance from her beginnings, from the unwanted, even despised, shadow-figure kept from sight in the darkened corners of her father's castle. Yet she was the same blind hunchback, a virtual dwarf, who walked with a limp, the very caricature of one who is least favored by heaven, scourged by the cruel hand of fate as few others have been.

The man of the world, viewing what he would have considered a monstrous figure feeling her way along the street, surely saw her as one abandoned not only by father and mother but by God Himself. The one true answer for him was not to come during the saint's life, but after her death.

Blessed Margaret died on April 13, 1320, when she was but thirty-three years of age. Her body rests exposed at the School for the Blind in Castello, clothed in the black and white habit of her order. The flesh is intact. The irony in this can scarcely escape our notice.

Though whole centuries have passed, her malformed body remains incorrupt, while throughout those same ages countless reigning beauties have faded, their comeliness vanished with the years, victim to the ravages of time.

THE GIFT OF TEARS

Arsenius

THE desert has long held for man a nearly indefinable attraction. Its appeal would appear to be beyond the limits of reason, for the desert by its very nature is a place deprived, a land without, barren of what other regions possess, of that which grows and flourishes and spreads. Barren of what *lives*, in a word, and, in living, draws other life to itself. So it is to fertile ground that man comes to settle and farm, to build city and factory, land where there is water, where there are trees for shade, and where there is grass for pasture. In fertile land there is all that he requires to sustain himself and those around him with the work of his hands; there is what can provide him with a life of comfort and even those luxuries he might desire.

In sharp contrast, the desert can answer few such needs, and those it may satisfy are hard to come by, wrested from rock and sand. It appears to be a place meant precisely to defy man, to test (and to tempt) him, to thwart his sense of power and so humble him—to remind him that he is creation as well as creator, and to show him his true stature when he is most in the grip of his human pride.

There is not simply the barrenness he finds about him. There is the immensity of space, his horizon unbroken save perhaps for the mountain far, far in the distance, so that a man seems to himself smaller just because of where he is, in the vastness of emptiness that surrounds him.

But it is the silence of the place that can most surprise, and often discomfit, when one first comes here, away from city streets. Though it might be expected, in a land so forsaken as this, the silence is probably deeper than any one has encountered or "heard" before, so great, in fact, that he is either put off and ill at ease—or learns wisdom from the stillness.

It is not without meaning, one may believe, that the incarnate Lord came to earth in an almost desert setting and during the hours, as the carol says, of a silent night. Such a silence no doubt had much to do with the profound mystery of that moment, with what it can tell us of Gift and Love that come when all around is empty and arid and with what can transpire just as the clamor of men dies away and the air for a brief while is still.

Nor should there be much wonder that some of the earliest Christians sought to follow Christ more perfectly by withdrawing to the solitude of the desert. If others came from the cities to seek them out, to ask for their counsel, it was to partake of the knowledge and wisdom these solitary men themselves had acquired in the quietude of their desert dwelling.

Among them was Saint Arsenius. He was of that brotherhood of men, beginning with Saint Anthony of the Desert, who took up their abode in the arid, unoccupied lands of Egypt. They were a new breed of holy men who, in such seemingly hostile places, appeared on the scene to base their rule of life on the Gospel.

For some, perhaps, the harsh environment in which they lived was no great change from what they had known before. They had grown used to what the desert offered, or did not offer, a man. But for Arsenius, who first appeared there when already in his middle years, the contrast to his previous life was truly stark.

He fled to the desert from the rich trappings of an emperor's court. Born around 354 in Rome, he was of senatorial rank and live in a style commensurate with his high office. He wore fine clothes. He resided in spacious quarters. He had a retinue of servants at his command.

The turning point in his life was to come, though he could not have been aware of it at the time, when he was appointed tutor to the two sons of Emperor Theodosius the Great of Constantinople. These sons, Arcadius and Honorius, were as it happened a dissolute pair, spoiled perhaps by pride in their royal lineage and more than a trial for someone given the formidable charge of instructing them. For one with a nature such as that possessed by Arsenius, they proved to be the most present, most visible, signs of an age and a style of life gone wrong. Even so, he served as their tutor for ten years, while his disquiet increased within him.

But his limit was at last reached. Out of his long disquiet had grown a desire for a retired life far from the intemperance and luxuriousness of the royal court. It was in the end a desire he could no longer deny, and at the age of forty he left the plush environment of palace life and fled Constantinople for Alexandria. There he joined some monks. But his past was not to be so easily shed as the fine clothing he had worn on his back. He was soon given the first test of his humility. The monks chided him; they nicknamed him the "Father of the Emperors" as a reminder of his history. He might flee the likes of Arcadius and Honorius. He might forever leave behind the rich food and elegant quarters of the castle. But in this place he could not rid himself of what he had been.

There was nothing for him to do but move still farther on, to where a man could strip himself wholly of his past. The choice seemed then an obvious one: the desert, the barren land that was itself shorn of all that had to do with the life he had known, a place scoured of everything but what was most essential.

So it was that this refugee from an emperor's court was next to be found with the monks who lived in the Egyptian desert area of Skete. He was first treated no better here than he had been in Alexandria. His humility was no less tested. The monks were either rude to the newcomer in their midst or ignored him entirely, to see if his apparent desire to reorder his life was of a passing nature or if he truly sought what might be found in their company.

He passed the test. The humbleness he displayed saw him through, and thus began the new life of Arsenius, palace tutor turned desert father, a saint of the silent land. The transformation was startling and entire. He wore the meanest of clothing, practiced rigorous penances, and engaged in constant prayer.

Thanks to the desert fathers, the arid land that was their home was fertile in one regard, and we need be eternally grateful for this flowering from out of so otherwise fruitless a soil. They possessed a unique form of simple wisdom, born perhaps from the austerity of their daily existence and from the time they had for contemplation, which was lacking to those still bound to the harsh business of making a living, the world of city and town, of trade and commerce. Thus, we are the heirs of this wisdom, the pithy sayings, the food for thought, the sage observations of men who, unfettered by the bonds of "civilized" life, got to the very root of things. Their words would make up a latter-day Book of Proverbs for those today who might wish to pause in their hurried lives and dwell upon what they could use to their soul's profit.

Saint Arsenius was no laggard here. He lived for more than half a century in the desert, and not without distilling from his own experience words to live by. One of his better-known maxims possesses an especially forceful ring, an insistent sound, in this modern culture of the television talk show, the daily round of ceaseless office chatter, the babble heard wherever a few have gathered, the gossip that passes for the day's news in the press. Almost as though it were meant for our ears, in this age of the communications revolution, Arsenius said: "I have often been sorry for having spoken, but never for having held my tongue."

The saint's highborn past would appear to have haunted him somewhat, now that he lived without things in the desert and was become in all matters a new man. For when he was informed that a relative who was well-to-do had died and left him all he possessed, Arsenius tore up the will, declaring: "I died before him and cannot be his heir."

In the same spirit of self-abasement, he took no pride in the knowledge he had acquired in his former life, the knowledge that had served him as educator, that learning which was to be found in the pages of books he had read or inside the walls of a schoolroom. Such "exterior learning", as he called it, "only puffs up the mind. I am not unacquainted with the learning of the Greeks and Romans," he went on to say, "but I have not yet learned the alphabet of the science of the saints." In this regard, he confessed, he needed a sense of his own "weakness, blindness, and insufficiency".

A man imbued with such a spirit, so apt to see the truth beneath the surface of things, was soon sought out by disciples,

some of whom would in turn become desert fathers themselves. Arsenius' response reveals another side to his nature, one
that some might judge less than saintly. For, when it came to
the question of surrounding himself with a company of men,
Arsenius proved to be a child of the desert altogether as much
as he was a desert father. The desert is all but defined by its
isolation, and for his part the saint kept to himself, shunning
others and seldom seeing strangers.

Yet for all this he was no misanthrope. Nor was he simply
shy, one who could claim he had lost his tongue after so many
years away from the association of men, the life of the street
and the city and the court. Far from having a dislike for men
or being shy, Arsenius had the greatest compassion for others.
It was simply a necessary choice, which he explained to others thus: "God knows how dearly I love you all. But I find I
cannot be both with God and with men at the same time.
Nor can I think of leaving God to converse with men."

The desert dweller who spent the whole night watching
and praying—that is to say, conversing with God—had no
time remaining for ordinary social pursuits. He could not be
at the same moment standing and upon his knees.

There is, however, one last facet to this saint's life that, in its
own striking way, overshadows all the rest that can be related
about him. Saint Arsenius, we are told by the Church, possessed the *gift of tears* to an unusual degree.

He who was said to be so blessed with the gift of tears wept
often and long over his own shortcomings and over those of
the world. His was a truly Christian anguish, but his tears
were no less real for that. The past too, his own past, moved
him to tears. It was reported he wept most ardently for
Arcadius and Honorius, the emperor's two inglorious sons,
whose souls he felt he had failed somehow to salvage. They

even now preyed on his mind, and he could not remain dry-eyed if he thought of their spiritual welfare.

So continually did he weep, we are told, that his tears wore away his eyelashes. This would further tell us a good deal about the love he bore his fellow man even though, as has been recounted, he kept to himself and guarded his solitude with the same ardor that caused him to lament his own state and the plight of mankind.

The tears shed by Arsenius never ceased flowing, up to the very last. He wept as he was dying, in his old age, and was asked if it was because he feared death. Another less honest soul might have denied he was now in the throes of such a human emotion. But he replied, "I am very afraid. Nor has this dread ever forsaken me from the time I first came into these deserts."

We are left, of course, to wonder at the full meaning of his words, whether the fear he so expressed was the common and understood fear of death itself or the fear that now he faced true and everlasting judgment before his Creator—he who so suffered from the thought of his own sins he was blessed with the gift of tears.

Whatever the cause for the last tears he shed, Arsenius was granted the grace of a holy death. He died in peace and filled with faith at ninety-five years of age.

THE STIGMATIC

Gemma Galgani

THROUGH all of mankind's history, so far as can be reckoned, the paranormal has drawn crowds of the curious, those attracted by what is beyond their experience, beyond what they can *know* to be reasonable and readily proven. The otherwise unexplainable is ever so much more seductive than the common, the everyday, which by its very nature one has got used to. It would appear to fill some human need for what is beyond the finite mind, the limits of reason.

A person watches, then, with a true fixation what he cannot really account for, thinking perhaps—just perhaps. . . . But can it actually be? Or is he the victim of some trick? Is he, when all is said and done, merely seeing things?

He may protest he has been tricked before. The conjurer is ever among us, with his magic act, performing his sleight-of-hand. Once deceived, a man will hold back, unwilling to believe even his eyes. But he cannot honestly be sure. In this manner is he cast about, never certain of one or the other for long, till he at last decides it is not for him either to affirm or to deny, and he shrugs and returns to the practical task at hand. He shall make no judgment either way, when there is enough to engage him that he can know and may verify.

The earnest religious seeker, on the other hand, cannot help but be one of those who is touched by what lies beyond his human grasp, what remains within the realm of the supernatural. For it is into this precise region that the religious pilgrim must venture, while the sceptic chooses to halt where he is and stay behind.

It is here, off the proven path, where the stigmatics are to be found, those who during their lives have borne what have been said to be the wounds of Christ on their bodies. Few have been more an object of interest, whether to the merely curious, to those looking for something exotic and out-of-the-way, or to those in all earnestness searching for some tangible sign to bolster their faith.

Saints have for the most part been ignored by the secular world during their lives. With few exceptions, they have not been widely recognized; more certainly they were not numbered among the powerful of the earth. Only the most faithful gathered about them. It is not sanctity that captures the eye of the masses or the ear of the press.

In the case of the stigmatic it is another matter, for better or worse. These are the ones who excite our interest, and not because of their piety or holiness, though both may be evident in abundance. It is rather because of the seemingly magical marks to be seen on their hands or their feet, or the wound, like that made by a soldier's lance, in their side. There have, of course, been stigmatics who, in the course of time, won the solemn respect of the public as well as its too-often morbid attention. In the Middle Ages there was Saint Francis of Assisi, who even during his lifetime was a force of great change for good in the world. More recently there was Blessed Padre Pio, the beloved Italian stigmatic, whose circle of devoted followers was spread far and wide, whose prayers were sought by thousands, and whose holiness is widely recognized.

But there have been others, and among the saints, who were neither so well known nor accorded a similar devotion or respect. They were thought to be erratic. Not only did they have the strange wounds to discomfit those about them, their behavior, too, perhaps at times further strained the credulity of the more sensible souls they encountered. Add one to the other, and the mix is too rich for the taste of many who might otherwise be found at their side.

One such stigmatic was Saint Gemma Galgani, a young woman from Tuscany of the late nineteenth century, who in the calendar of saints is described as a "quiet and unexcitable girl", but who nevertheless "was endowed with a remarkably fervent religious disposition". She cannot be considered an easy study, then, and it is not difficult to believe that during her few years of life she was scoffed at even while she won earnest attention.

Gemma was born in 1878, and not under happy circumstances. She was born into poverty and ill health. From early on she suffered from tuberculosis of the spine. This illness thwarted her desire as a young woman to become a Passionist nun. Because of her poor health she could not be admitted into the order.

She was not to be easily dissuaded. She began a series of novenas to Saint Gabriel, whom she reportedly saw in an apparition, and she was cured. Then she again sought to join the order but was once more rejected.

Shortly thereafter, in June 1899, she received the stigmata on her hands and feet. She bore the marks of Christ's crucifixion intermittently for some eighteen months, until early 1901. Later she was said to have received the marks of His scourging. The appearance of these painful wounds was accompanied by visions and ecstasies, all attested to by her confessor and spiritual director, Father Germano. She was to declare that, at those moments of true fervor, Jesus was corporally present.

Her mystical life was, however, not entirely beatific. Some of what she experienced was of another sort. The young stigmatic said she was a victim of assaults by the devil. While she endured these demonic attacks, she engaged in behavior that was demonic in itself. She once spat on a crucifix and broke her rosary beads.

This kind of physical attack by the devil is even farther from our ordinary human experience than are ecstasies and visions. Today, especially, we rarely hear anything about the reality of the devil, even as some abstract "spirit of evil", either in the street or from the pulpit. We have, in our thoroughly modern sophistication, outgrown any such concept of a real-life Satan, though we may still seem fascinated on occasion, perhaps in the case of a horror story, with the idea of the demonic. Yet a much-admired Catholic saint, the Curé d'Ars, as well as the stigmatic Padre Pio were both physically set upon by a very real devil, according to competent witnesses in each case. These witnesses reported sounds of struggle in the night, from the room to which the Curé had retired or from the cell occupied by Padre Pio. Both men appeared in the morning marked by bruises such as those sustained in a physical contest with something—or someone. Thus the experience related by Gemma Galgani was not wholly unique. But the reports of such assaults as these upon her could only add to her already controversial reputation. Through it all she maintained a spirit of peace and love. Following a long and painful illness, she died on Holy Saturday, April 11, 1903, at the age of only twenty-five.

A cultus sprang up about her almost at once. She was beatified in 1933, despite some opposition, as might be expected, and canonized in 1940.

The last word, as it happens, has still to be spoken on the wounds Gemma Galgani bore on her body. The Congregation of Rites pointed only to her "heroic virtues" in proclaiming her to be among the Communion of Saints. No judgment was forthcoming on the stigmata. That this was so is scarcely surprising. The Church has always been cautious in such matters, choosing not to rush in where she cannot clearly see the way, as in this case, where there is no substantial store of evidence to certify that the stigmata were of a supernatural origin. Some scholars have judged the appearance of the wounds to be the result of an emotional state experienced by the stigmatic. Others simply remain mystified by the phenomenon.

What are we to believe, then, about stigmatics? Are they true signs for the faithful, visible bearers of Our Lord's wounds? May they be sought out by those who for the moment are cast down in doubt?

The Church has said only that believing the stigmata to be from supernatural causes is not an article of faith. There is no inherent relationship, she has seen fit to point out, between sanctity and stigmatization.

Here the matter now rests. We are thus left to observe the strange marks and to wonder—to marvel at the lives of saints such as Gemma Galgani and to think that the visible wounds they bore, though they may never be fully explained, were meant to remind a heedless world of the suffering Christ. For who, after all, can read the mind of God?

THE POET

Robert Southwell

THE poet has seldom, if ever, been "one of us". The public throughout history has looked upon him as uncommon, probably eccentric: the outsider. But neither has he been thought of as a saint, some of whom might have as easily been described as uncommon, in their own way odd, and surely not readily received or understood. No, the poet has more likely been regarded, not as saint, but as sinner.

This would appear all but a requirement for the practice of his vocation. He must, after all, in the mind of the crowd, experience the full measure of both the pleasures and the depravity that life has to offer if he is, by word, to share with others a true sense of the heights and the depths of existence to which man can rise or descend. He is bound, or doomed, to taste of the fruit of the tree of evil if he is to define for us in his verse either its bitter taste or its sweetness. It cannot be otherwise, or else his work will be void of the authentic tone, the sure passion, that is demanded of it.

This would hardly allow the poet to live out his days as would his uncommon fellow, the saint, who for his part must wage his daily inner battle to conquer those same human

97

furies that would ensnare him on the path he has taken toward sanctity. So it is that the saint has not the "excuse" of living the profligate life all for his art's sake—the sanction we would grant to the poet.

In this view the poet by nature allows himself to be used as instrument by whatever force, evil or not, that will make possible the creation of some greater good: the art he produces or verse he composes, which, if it be true and lasting, speaks for every man, everywhere, through all time, from the depth of his soul. Thus it is the world's cry that is uttered, its lament, its rage or romantic fervor or joy, that we hear sounded by another whose feelings we share but whose talent for expression we lack.

The image of the poet as free spirit, unbound by custom, unfettered by any regard for common morality—this is the likeness passed down to us, whether stereotypical, and so distorted, or not. There comes to mind, as representative, the two Frenchmen François Rabelais and François Villon, the first called a master of the grotesque, the second a vagabond poet often jailed and once even condemned to death. Or what of the English romantic poet Lord Byron, his years of dissipation, his failed marriage, the exile who died in Italy at thirty-six. More modern examples might include the suicidal poets. The American Hart Crane, a driven man at odds with his world throughout his short life, ended that life when he jumped from a steamer in the Gulf of Mexico in 1932. That same year was born another American poet, Sylvia Plath, acclaimed by the critics for her creative fire and the intensity of her verse, who had first attempted suicide when she was nineteen and later died by her own hand, in London, in 1963.

The renowned Welsh poet Dylan Thomas, doubtless a man of genius to the core, can be remembered as roaring drunkenly onto some university or public stage where he had been brought while on tour in this country to recite his work. Thomas, too, died the proverbial younger poet. But his years were cut short by his dissolute days and nights. His was no suicidal end. Thomas had a clear aversion to death.

Surely, we are reminded, this demon-possessed modern-day poet spoke for many in this present world in penning one of his most quoted verses:

> Do not go gentle into that good night,
> Old age should burn and rave at close of day;
> Rage, rage against the dying of the light.

So, it is said, the fallen poet says for others what they, as common and law-abiding and typically moral men, might think but not have the gift to put into words.

This picture of the poet as debaucher, as has been noted, may be false or exaggerated, but few would deny that it is the conventional one. The underlying truth of the image is made more startlingly clear by the fact that the greatest exceptions to the rule—in this case, the Christian poets—so stand out from among their peers as to be all but "scandalous" in their own way!

There need only be called for witness T. S. Eliot, the proper and intellectual English poet who, once he had caught the attention of the literary world with *The Wasteland*, in his later life became, in his own words, "an Anglo-Catholic in religion, a classicist in literature, and a royalist in politics". And in these same years he produced the religious classics *Ash Wednesday*, *Journey of the Magi*, and *Four Quartets*. Then there is Gerard Manley Hopkins, the Jesuit priest and a major poet of the nineteenth century. Hopkins, wholly unrecognized during his lifetime (not one of his poems was published while he lived), is today regarded as a foremost poet of his age, though not one whose verse is easily read or understood.

Though probably neither of these two estimable literary figures was a poet-saint, one who could claim both crowns is Saint John of the Cross. This prime mystic of the Catholic faith has also been called, in more than one instance, the greatest poet Spain has produced. There can be little doubt of his creative power. But it seems that for the litterateur the saint's poetry is so fused with his prose, as appendage or accompaniment, that the one has become lost in the shadow of the other.

In this mystic's *Living Flame of Love*, for example, the prose of the book "merely" serves to define, or expand upon, the poet's four "Stanzas of the Soul", the lines that introduce the work. Whatever the reason, Saint John of the Cross is most often regarded as saint, not as poet, his verse obscured by the attraction of the holy man and his vision.

Rather, it is to a lesser-known sanctified soul and verse-maker to whom we would turn if we are to define the poet-saint as one acknowledged equally as true poet and true saint, the first by literary circles, the second by the Church. This would be Blessed Robert Southwell, a sixteenth-century Jesuit priest, who, while he was in the end cruelly tortured and martyred for the faith in England, yet managed during his brief lifetime to write verse that was, and is, accorded its rightful place in past and present literary annals.

Southwell's gift as poet was attested to by no less a literary figure than Ben Jonson, critic and dramatist often ranked near to Shakespeare in stature, who declared he would be content to destroy many of his own lines should he have been allowed to compose Southwell's brief allegory "The Burning Babe". In this poem, one of his better-known verses, Southwell tells of a winter night when he stood in the snow and a "pretty babe all burning bright did in the air appear". The babe, who "floods of tears did shed", cries because "none approach to warm their hearts or feel my fire but I!"

In this vein the poem continues, to the end:

> With this he vanished out of sight
> And swiftly shrunk away—
> And straight I called unto my mind
> That it was Christmas Day.[1]

The author of such religious sentiments was no more common in those days than in these, and the anthologist Louis Untermeyer, in *A Treasury of Great Poems, English and American*, has written of Southwell and his contemporaries: "Among the groups of courtiers and the rabble of rowdies, Robert Southwell stands out strangely, a fanatic spirit, like a portrait of a gaunt zealot painted by El Greco."[2]

The description is apt, if one is to judge from a crayon drawing of the poet-saint produced from an oil portrait now lost. It is a memorable face, etched with rough lines, yet that of a man not given to ordinary thoughts or common pleasures. The close-cropped hair, the rawboned cheeks, the long thin nose and dark eyes—all add to the look indeed of a "fanatic spirit" or "gaunt zealot", who might well, as happened, be both a true poet and a bloodied martyr for the right cause.

The life of Robert Southwell was not long. It was, however, intense, not so much to be measured in years as in the ardor with which those years were lived out and the courage and sanctity shown as they ended.

He was born in Norfolk, England, around 1561. Though his mother remained a staunch Catholic, his father wavered with the times, more than once changing both his religious

---

[1] *A Treasury of Great Poems, English and American*, ed. Louis Untermeyer (New York: Simon and Schuster, 1955), 245.

[2] Ibid., 244.

and political affiliations. Robert was sent to school at Douay in France, to be educated by the Jesuits, possibly because his father was a Catholic at that juncture, or simply because of the school's reputation. He then went to Paris, where, at the early age of seventeen, he expressed a desire to join the Society of Jesus. He was at first judged to be too young for membership in the religious order and, in his sorrow at this turn of events, was said to have written his first verses.

But, not of a nature to be easily dissuaded, the young Robert walked to Rome, where his persistence was rewarded, and he became a Jesuit novice in 1578. He was ordained in 1584 and sent as missionary-priest to England, not without some awareness of what he might face, for the Jesuit General had said of those who were dispatched to those shores that it was as if he were "sending lambs to the slaughter".

Southwell, for a fact, was soon to be swept up in the savage persecution of Catholics in England. In 1592 he was betrayed and arrested, jailed for three years, during which time he underwent terrible torture, and finally was hanged, drawn, and quartered on February 21, 1595. He was thirty-three at the time of his death, the same age as Christ at His crucifixion.

With a few lines, then, if that were the sum of it, the life of Robert Southwell could be recounted, much as it might be reported in the usual obituary on some back page of a newspaper today. But he was poet as well as martyr, and a poet's words can outlast the man, endure beyond his own few years on earth.

Thus we are given not only the bounty of his verse but what can well be considered his masterwork, pages left us to encourage and inspire all those of any time or place who are asked to suffer, even to death, for the faith: Southwell's stirring poetic-prose primer for martyrs, *An Epistle of Comfort.*

This work, we can believe, blossomed only after the poet

had given thought to the matter over the years. For we are told that Southwell felt early on he would be a martyr. And he did not discount what this meant, what could well lie in store for him, a fugitive Catholic priest. He knew of the dread sufferings of Edmund Campion, another Jesuit martyr-saint caught up in the same anti-Catholic fury then sweeping through the corridors of power in England. But he did not cower before the grim prospect of such a fearsome future for himself. The poet wrote to the General of the Jesuit Order: "Nor do I so much dread the tortures as look forward to the crown."

His own martyrdom, however, was not to occur before he was allowed to use his considerable mastery of the language to offer solace to, and exhort, those persecuted believers whom he served as priest and counselor. In an early homily, which has been preserved as "Mary Magdalen's Funeral Tears", he refers to God's love and assures those oppressed or maltreated that "no difficulty can stay it, no impossibility appal it."

Such sentiments, in a real sense, had to be expressed "on the run" by a priest who was more likely than not but one step ahead of the religious police of the day, who was forced to spend much time in the simple act of hiding out. On occasion he assumed various disguises to conceal his true identity, in the best adventure-story tradition. It was a role that was entirely out of character for one described as so gentle and quiet a man as Blessed Robert.

This contrast between the life he was compelled to endure and that promised in the City of God was to become a central theme for Southwell. That is to say: the Christian paradox. The Christian is to give up all to gain all. He will sell all that he possesses to have what alone is worth possessing. He will give up his life in order to gain it.

The saint would write:

> I live, but such a life as ever dies;
> I die, but such a death as never ends.

This, of course, makes no earthly sense! But for Southwell it not only summed up true wisdom, it was the source for poetic inspiration as well.

Much of his poetry was written, necessarily, while he was in prison, when he was not obliged to live the life of a renegade. In assuming the role of poet as a part of his religious vocation, Southwell was indeed destined to stand out from the literary crowd, from "among the groups of courtiers and the rabble of rowdies".

The saint seems not unaware of this, of the near singular place of the religious poet. But he would put the tool of the poets to his own use. Or, as he said, he wished "to weave a new web in their own loom".

Southwell decried the fact that so great a number of his contemporaries put to a profane use, unworthy of their calling, the gift for verse they so clearly possessed. The poet's gift, for a man such as Southwell, could not help but require a Giver for whose honor and glory he, at least, would pen his brief and fervid lyrics, filled with spiritual passion, as well as his longer poetic works.

His long narrative poem *Saint Peter's Complaint* portrays the last days of Christ as told by a remorseful Prince of the Apostles. While Southwell hoped to be remembered chiefly for this verse, it is for his shorter, emotionally laden lyrics he is best known.

But it is with a work of prose that the poet-saint most clearly and ardently speaks for the Church to her faithful today. It is a book whose pages are filled with a poetic prose brilliant in metaphor, phrasing, and allusion, a book that sums up what was for Southwell, as has been noted, his primary message, the Christian paradox—the frail nature of all worldly happiness and pleasure and the true spiritual joy that may most surely be found in the very midst of suffering. This has come to us as *An Epistle of Comfort*, addressed to the Catholic martyrs of his day in England. But its words, because they are based upon enduring truths, might well have been directed to those faithful of this, or any, age who are called upon to give their lives in exchange for that joy which the poet, himself soon to be martyred, holds forth as the prize.

The work grew out of a few spiritual letters Southwell had written to Blessed Philip Howard, one of the condemned who was imprisoned in the Tower at the time and in whose home he lived or was given shelter. Southwell wished to strengthen the will of his friend, to encourage him in his confinement, to make somehow more bearable the physical suffering he might be undergoing. This was the simple and personal beginning of a book that became a classic work addressed to all such martyrs. Here he writes: "What can there be in life, either durable or very delightsome, when life itself is so frail and fickle a thing?" Thus it is that "every day we die, and hourly lose some part of our life; even when we grow, we decrease."

Life, then, as "frail and fickle", is thereby exchangeable. But for what? Certainly not for something of lesser, or even something of simply equal, value. And indeed not, when it is the lives of the martyrs that are involved—those martyrs who, as part of any exchange to be offered, face a death at once brutal and painful.

In order that they might hold out till the end, Southwell asks that they think of "the majesty of their souls" in heaven:

> For first of all the comforts, joys and delights that are here scattered in divers creatures and countries, all the beauty and comeliness that any worldly being here hath, shall there be

united and joined together in every saint and they shall be without any of those imperfections wherewithal they are here coped.

This is the "crown" that awaits them, of which the poet had formerly spoken. The fearful torture cannot last, but they shall wear the crown forever. And in a forceful manner, by citing example, Southwell sets forth to confirm his case in contrasting with the martyr's redemptive death the fate suffered by those who, in the earliest days of the Church, so savagely ended the lives of the first brave witnesses to the faith.

One, he writes, has only to

consider what reward hath been given to such as persecuted God's flock. . . .

Nero, the ring-leader of your dance, fell from killing Christians to be his own butcher and, murdering himself, he ended his life with these words: *Filthily have I lived, and more filthily do I die.* Domitian was stabbed to death by his own servants. Maximinus was slain together with his children. . . . Decius tasted of the same cup, seeing his children slain and himself with them. . . . Diocletian, after many diseases, in the end consuming away, fell mad and killed himself, and his house was burnt up with fire from heaven.

The dreary list goes on at some length, bearing the names of those cruel tyrants who, as the poet wishes to stress, met their own harsh and torturous fate but without the lasting crown that is reserved for the martyr. God, for Southwell, is not mocked on earth. He who has declared "Vengeance is mine" acts in history to make good His claim.

In his verses the poet of any age declares himself. He discloses for others his innermost thoughts and feelings: what he sees and knows and believes and, now by word, affirms of the life and the world around him. It is his private vision made public and put to paper for others, most of them utter strangers, to share. In this sense *An Epistle of Comfort* is a book-length prose poem composed by Southwell, not only because of the poetic language found on its pages but because of the fervor of its content. Every page is marked with the fire of its poet-author. The book is meant to move the reader, to stir his very heart and soul, to confirm his resolve to give even his life for what is more than, and beyond, that life itself.

Southwell here then, for his part, allows himself no retreat. He had anticipated that he, too, would be martyred. Now, as poet, he was on record. He had spoken, for all to hear. He could not then, with so great an ardor, admonish others to hold fast in the face of so brutal an end, if he were afterward to recant his words when his own moment came to suffer as they had, to stand where they had once stood.

"I live, but such a life as ever dies. . . ." So he had written in another place.

The saint had not long to wait for his own Golgotha, one that would in truth put his bold words to the test. Betrayed (as was his Lord) and arrested, he was imprisoned for three years, during which time he was mercilessly and repeatedly tortured. As for his courage shown during such moments of great trial, we have the report of a fellow priest who called Blessed Robert a "Goliath of fortitude".

So the poet died. So the saint lives on. For this we have the word of the poet, who at the conclusion of *An Epistle of Comfort* declared: "In sum, not he who beginneth, but he who persevereth unto the end, shall be saved."

BIBLIOGRAPHY

Bernanos, Georges. *The Last Essays of Georges Bernanos*. Translated by Joan and Barry Ulanov. Chicago: Henry Regnery, 1955.

Bonniwell, O.P., William R. *The Life of Blessed Margaret of Castello*. Rockford, Ill.: TAN Books and Publishers, 1983.

Butler, Alban. *Butler's Lives of the Saints*. Edited, revised, and supplemented by Herbert Thurston, S.J., and Donald Atwater. New York: P. J. Kenedy and Sons, 1962.

Englebert, Omer. *The Lives of the Saints*. New York: Barnes and Noble, 1994.

Ghéon, Henri. *The Secret of the Curé d'Ars*. Translated by F. J. Sheed. New York: Sheed and Ward, 1938.

John of the Cross, Saint. *Living Flame of Love*. Translated by E. Allison Peers. New York: Image Books, 1962.

Lives of the Saints. New York: Catholic Book Publishing, 1993.

Mauriac, François. *The Son of Man*. Translated by Bernard Murchland. Cleveland and New York: World Publishing, 1960.

Monro, Margaret T. *Blessed Margaret Clitherow*. London: Burns, Oates, and Washbourne, 1948.

The Norton Anthology of Poetry. Fourth edition. Edited by Mary Ferguson, Mary Jo Salter, and Jon Stallworthy. New York: W. W. Norton, 1996.

Southwell, Robert. *An Epistle of Comfort*. Edited by Margaret Waugh. London: Burns and Oates, 1966.

A Treasury of Great Poems, English and American. Edited by Louis Untermeyer. New York: Simon and Schuster, 1955.

Walsh, James A. *A Modern Martyr: Théophane Vénard*. New York: Catholic Foreign Mission Society of America, 1913.